سورة الفرقان

SOORAH AL-FURQAAN
CHAPTER 25 OF THE NOBLE QURAN

RESOURCES FOR YOUR 30-DAY STUDY
OF THE COMMENTARY OF AL-IMAM AS-SA'DEE
WORKBOOK PREPARED BY: MOOSAA RICHARDSON

THIS COPY BELONGS TO:

First Print (Paperback) Edition: Rajab 1445 (February 2024)

Richardson, Moosaa. (Author)

Harding, Gibril (Proofreader)

Soorah al-Furqaan, Chapter 25 of the Noble Quran (Workbook) / Resources For Your 30-Day Study of the Commentary of al-Imam as-Sa'dee

ISBN: 979-8879511963

1. Nonfiction —Religion —Islam —Koran & Sacred Writings.

2. Nonfiction —Religion —Islam —General.

3. Nonfiction —Religion —Islam —Sunnism.

TABLE OF CONTENTS

The First Muslim Mosque (Al-Masjid Al-Awwal), est. 1932, located in the heart of Pittsburgh's historic Hill District, hosts a vibrant community of local and international congregants, adhering to the tenants of Orthodox Sunni/Salafi Islam, actively condemning terrorist organizations such as ISIS, Alqaeda, and the (so-called) Muslim Brotherhood.

TWITTER: @1MMPGH

WEBSITE: WWW.FIRSTMUSLIMMOSQUE.COM

EMAIL: INFO@FIRSTMUSLIMMOSQUE.COM

PREFACE

All praise is due to Allah, the Lord, Creator, and Sustainer of all things. He alone possesses the sovereign dominion of the heavens and the earth; He has not begotten any son, nor does He have any partner in that dominion. He created everything and decreed it all with precise measure, and thus none deserve any worship other than Him. It is He who sent down the Furqaan, the Criterion between right and wrong (the Quran), to His noble worshipper, Muhammad ibn 'Abdillaah (may Allah raise his rank and grant him peace), so His Book would be a warning to the entire creation and a guide to success in this life and the Hereafter, when our Lord arrives along with the angels, rank upon rank!

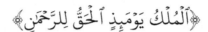

"All sovereignty on that Day is rightfully owned by *ar-Rahmaan* (the Most Gracious)." [25:26]

It provides comfort to the heart, tranquility to the soul, and relaxation to the chest that Allah connects the sovereignty on the Day of Judgment to His Name, ar-Rahmaan (the Most Gracious), the One whose Mercy encompasses all things, covers all living beings, fills the entire universe, and regulates this life and the Next. By it, every shortcoming is compensated for, and every deficiency departs. The Names which indicate it (Mercy) outnumber the Names indicating His Anger. His Mercy precedes His Anger and overtakes it, so it (Mercy) has precedence and dominance. He created this weak human being, honored him, and bestowed His Grace upon him, in order to complete His Favor upon him, and in order to cover him in His Mercy. When they arrive at a place of humility, surrender, and dire need, in front of Him [on the Day of Judgment], awaiting His Verdict upon them and worried about what might happen to them, He is more Merciful to them than they are to their own selves, [more Merciful to them] than their own parents! *So what do you think He will do with them?* No one is ruined with Allah other than an utterly destroyed person. No one could be outside of His Mercy other than one determined to be eternally miserable, one upon whom the word of punishment is actualized! [1]

May Allah save us from His Punishment and grant us His Mercy and Forgiveness!

As for what follows: It is from the great favors of our Lord that we -once again- prepare for the blessed month of Ramadhaan, *in shaa' Allah*.

For many of us, these **"Ramadhaan Lessons"** have become an essential part of our experience, and I am -once again- humbled and honored to be part of your days and nights, asking Allah to accept from me and all of you. To briefly recount some of the many beautiful favors of Allah upon us over the last few years, as it relates to these lessons:

Volume 1 of this series was our study tool for the classes in Ramadhaan 1439 (2018). Thirty lessons consisted of seven modules each, with Grammar, *Tafseer*, and *Hadeeth* modules, as well as a variety of extension activities, beginning with the verses about fasting.

---

[1] *Tayseer al-Kareem ar-Rahmaan*, in explanation of *Soorah al-Furqaan*, Verse 26.

Volume 2 (1440/2019) included fifteen *Tafseer* lessons and fifteen *Hadeeth* lessons on various topics. A *fatwa* from Shaykh Ibn Baaz (may Allah have Mercy on him) was included in each lesson.

Volume 3 (1441/2020) included 30 lessons on each of the four main topics: *Tafseer, Hadeeth,* Arabic, and *Tajweed.* The 30 verses of **Soorah al-Mulk** were studied, one verse a day, for each day of the month, from **four** different books of *Tafseer*! Brief lessons in *Tajweed* and Arabic were also included.

Volume 4 (1442/2021) included another set of 120 lessons in *Tafseer, Hadeeth,* Arabic (*Sarf,* or word derivatives and conjugations), and *Tajweed,* focused on **Soorah Ibraaheem**. We cut back to reading **two** (not four) books of *Tafseer* – **al-Baghawee** and **as-Sa'dee**.

Volume 5 (1443/2022) included two lessons a day in study of **Soorah Ghaafir**, from those same two books of *Tafseer*.

Last year's lessons (1444/2023) included daily lessons in study of **Soorah al-Israa'**, reading the explanation of al-Imam as-Sa'dee (may Allah have Mercy on him).

All six of the previous workbooks remain available on Amazon and at many Islamic bookstores in different parts of the world, and to Allah Alone is the praise. Furthermore, the recordings from all those activities remain easily and freely accessible at al-Masjid al-Awwal's public radio station:

▶ ***www.Spreaker.com/user/radio1mm***

WHAT TO EXPECT IN THIS YEAR'S LESSONS

This workbook and this year's Ramadhaan 1445 (2024) classes will be a study of the amazing 25th chapter of the Quran, **Soorah al-Furqaan**. Following last year's precedent, we will maintain a similar focus and scope throughout the lessons and workbook this year, *in shaa' Allah*, with 30 *Tafseer* lessons in total. Compared to the much larger content of the first five volumes of the Ramadhaan Lessons, this more refined scope can rightfully be described as: "Less is more!"

1. MORE FOCUS ON AL-IMAM AS-SA'DEE

Our focused study of only one book of *Tafseer* allows us to zoom in a little more than we normally would, getting more of a feel for the style and methodology of the amazing explanation of the great scholar, **al-Imam 'Abdur-Rahmaan ibn Naasir as-Sa'dee** (may Allah have Mercy on him).

2. LIVE DAILY BROADCASTS

As you expect from us, we provide live daily sessions throughout the month of Ramadhaan, broadcast right from our beloved masjid in Pittsburgh, the First Muslim Mosque, *in shaa' Allah*. The high-quality MP3 recordings of our live classes remain available for those who could not attend, to listen in whenever that is easy. *(Check out the easy visual guide on page 10, and on the back cover.)*

3. WEEKLY QUIZZES AND A FINAL EXAM

Following last year's precedent, this year's workbook also includes weekly quizzes and a final exam. After each week of lessons, you will have an opportunity to review and evaluate your understanding of that week's classes with a 10-question multiple-choice quiz, *in shaa' Allah*. Additionally, a 25-question comprehensive final exam is available. These resources, along with a complete answer key, are found on **pages 73-84** of this workbook. (The answer key is found on **page 93**.)

4. A PERSONAL PROGRESS TRACKER

To help you manage all these resources and stay on track throughout the month, our uniquely designed **Personal Progress Tracker** provides more structure to your study. With it, you can track your daily progress and weekly quiz scores, *in shaa' Allah*. Adding in your final exam score after you review the month's lessons, you will get a total score out of 100 points. This helpful tool is found on **page 12** of this workbook.

SOME OF THE MAIN THEMES OF *SOORAH AL-FURQAAN*

The *soorah* opens with the phrase, **"tabaaraka,"** translated simply as, **"Blessed is He,"** which is explained by al-Imam as-Sa'dee (may Allah have Mercy on him) as: "His Greatness is manifest, His Descriptions are perfect, and His Kindness is abundant." This unique and powerful phrase is repeated two more times in the *soorah*, in Verses 10 and 61. About this, al-Imam as-Sa'dee (may Allah have Mercy on him) said:

> This *soorah* includes meanings that demonstrate His Greatness, the vastness of His Sovereignty, the absolute enactment of His Will, the all-encompassing scope of His Knowledge and Capability, the all-inclusive nature of His Dominion, as it relates to His commands and verdicts of recompense, and the completeness of His Wisdom. It also includes what demonstrates the expansiveness of His Mercy, how far-reaching His Generosity is, and His abundant Kindness in both this world and the Next. Considering these meanings, the repetition of this beautiful description (*"tabaaraka"*) is befitting.[2]

Similar to other early Makkan chapters of the Quran, *Soorah al-Furqaan* includes a heavy focus on the Hereafter, defense of the honesty and character of the Prophet (may Allah raise his rank and grant him peace), emphasis on the significance of the revelation of the Quran and its guidance, clarifications of the purpose of life, descriptions of the believers and disbelievers, as well as vivid descriptions of Paradise and the Hellfire. The foolishness of many of the demands of the disbelievers is also exposed. Many of Allah's Names and beautiful descriptions of His perfect Attributes are found throughout the *soorah* as well.

A DETAILED GUIDE TO PERFECTING ONE'S CHARACTER

Making it especially impactful in Ramadhaan, this *soorah* equips us with an amazing guide to attaining the pinnacle of upright Islamic character, explaining how we might reach the lofty rank of *'Ebaad ar-Rahmaan*, the true slave-servants of the Most Gracious, in Verses 65-74. These Verses make up the major focus of our last ten nights this Ramadhaan, *in shaa'*

---

[2] *Tayseer al-Kareem ar-Rahmaan*, in explanation of *Soorah al-Furqaan*, Verse 61.

Allah. Al-Imam as-Sa'dee summarizes the descriptions of these great worshippers (may Allah make us from them) by saying: In summary, Allah describes them with:

1. Tranquility and calmness
2. Humility unto Him
3. Humility with His worshippers
4. Good manners
5. Forbearance
6. Depth of good character
7. Pardoning the ignorant
8. Not accompanying the ignorant
9. Graceful responses to bad treatment
10. Praying at night
11. Sincerity in that [prayer]
12. Fear of Hell
13. Begging Allah for protection from Hell
14. Fulfillment of financial obligations
15. Giving optional charity
16. Balance in spending
17. Moderation in all matters
18. Avoidance of major sins
19. Sincerity in all their worship
20. Refraining from physical harm
21. Respect of people's honor
22. Repentance
23. Absence from gatherings of evil speech
24. Distance from evil speech [themselves]
25. Refraining from frivolity
26. Personal integrity
27. Altruistic empathy for others
28. Distance from disgraceful behavior
29. Submission to Allah's Verses
30. Understanding the meanings of the Quran
31. Implementation of the Quran
32. Diligence in applying Quranic rulings
33. Supplicating for one's family
34. Diligence in teaching one's family
35. Offering good religious reminders
36. Sincere advice to one's family
37. Aspiring to be leading examples of piety[3]

WHY NOT USE THE KHAN/HILALI TRANSLATION OF MEANINGS: "THE NOBLE QURAN"?

Since the translation of the meanings of the Noble Quran by Khan and Hilali is the best one available in the English language, one might be curious to know why we did not use it for *Soorah al-Furqaan* in our workbook. To understand our choice, one must understand the complexities of translating the meanings of the Quran. The Quran is the miraculous and amazing Speech of Allah. Sometimes, a Verse has more than one angle of intended meaning, which requires a translator to choose one of them in how he/she will represent that in the translated expression. Some choices made by Khan/Hilali simply do not match the choices of al-Imam as-Sa'dee. Four examples of such differences in interpretation are as follows:

Verse 4: Khan/Hilali interpreted the description of injustice and falsehood to be a continuation of the accusations of the disbelievers, while al-Imam as-Sa'dee interpreted that as Allah's rebuke of the disbelievers, people of injustice and lies.

Verse 24: Khan/Hilali chose to represent the Arabic phrase of *ism at-tafdheel* in two places as "the best" and "the fairest," whereas al-Imam as-Sa'dee made it a point to explain the comparative nature of the phrase, as opposed to their superlative translation. This same difference appears again in the translation of Verse 34.

Verse 74: Khan/Hilali translated the meaning of *"azwaaj"* to be **"wives,"** while as-Sa'dee chose to interpret this as a broader idea, those similar, or mates, and then he explained that wives are from the generality of that.

Verse 75: Khan/Hilali interpreted the word *"salaam"* as "the word of peace and respect," while as-Sa'dee explained it as "safety and freedom from all harms and deficiencies."

---

[3] *Tayseer al-Kareem ar-Rahmaan*, in explanation of *Soorah al-Furqaan*, Verse 75.

HOW TO ACCESS THE RECORDINGS

Go to **www.Spreaker.com/user/radio1mm** on your computer, phone, or smart device, and then scroll down on the main page under the title, **"PODCASTS"**. Click on **"1445 (2024) Ramadhaan Lessons,"** and you will then see a list of all available class recordings. Save the page's location or create a shortcut to it, so you can return to it easily. There is an easy visual guide which demonstrates exactly how you can access these free online classes on **page 10**.

PRINT OR ELECTRONIC VERSION?

These workbooks have been prepared to accompany our courses as traditionally printed paperback workbooks, available in hardcover editions as well. They have been adapted, secondarily, as Kindle print replicas and in PDF format. This is primarily for our brothers and sisters in different parts of the world who follow the classes but cannot obtain the printed versions in their location. Others may prefer the electronic versions, as they have devices which allow notetaking. Without a device that allows easy notetaking, we highly recommend the print versions of the workbooks (paperback or hardcover).

As you most likely already know, **our workbooks have not been designed for independent self-study.** To achieve the intended benefit from these lessons, attend our free online classes daily, or listen to the recordings whenever that is easy for you, and follow along using this workbook.

May Allah reward my ever-supportive wife and family, my beloved community at the First Muslim Mosque of Pittsburgh, my respected companion, Gibril Harding, for his helpful review, my Patreon community, and all of those who study with us and support these efforts, wherever they may be. I ask Allah that He grant me and all of you success in attaining His Pleasure and in drawing near to Him. May He raise the rank of his Messenger, Muhammad, and grant him and his family and companions peace.

(Asking Allah to make this a blessed month for you.)

ABUL-'ABBAAS
MOOSAA RICHARDSON
Education Director
First Muslim Mosque
Pittsburgh, Pennsylvania
Email: MR@bakkah.net
Twitter: @1MMeducation

HOW TO ACCESS THE FREE CLASS RECORDINGS & AUDIO RESOURCES

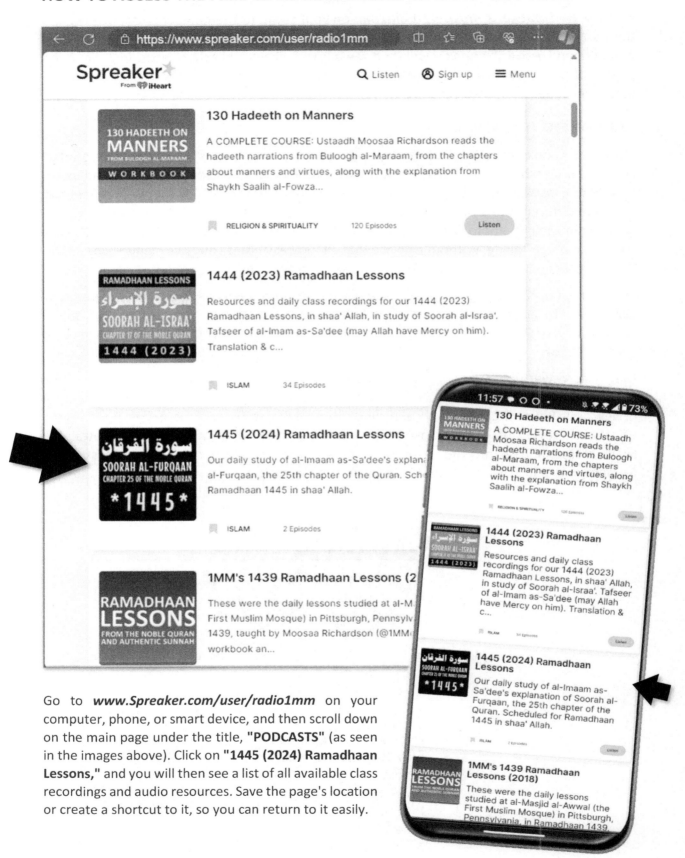

Go to **www.Spreaker.com/user/radio1mm** on your computer, phone, or smart device, and then scroll down on the main page under the title, **"PODCASTS"** (as seen in the images above). Click on **"1445 (2024) Ramadhaan Lessons,"** and you will then see a list of all available class recordings and audio resources. Save the page's location or create a shortcut to it, so you can return to it easily.

INTRODUCTION

ABOUT THE SOORAH

1. Its names, general theme & main topics
2. Is it *Makkee* or *Madanee*? And what is the difference?

ABOUT THESE LESSONS

3. Who was as-Sa'dee?
4. About the *Tafseer* of as-Sa'dee
5. About these daily lessons

Serious students may use the following *Personal Progress Tracker* to monitor their completion of the course, as explained on page 7, in the *Preface*. Students who complete the course are encouraged to go back and review their memorization and understanding of the entire text every six months or so.

DAY	FOCUS OF STUDY	STUDIED	MEMORIZED	SCORE
PERSONAL PROGRESS TRACKER				
1	SOORAH AL-FURQAAN VERSES 1-2	☐ 0.5	☐ 0.5	___ / 1
2	SOORAH AL-FURQAAN VERSES 3-4	☐ 0.5	☐ 0.5	___ / 1
3	SOORAH AL-FURQAAN VERSES 5-6	☐ 0.5	☐ 0.5	___ / 1
4	SOORAH AL-FURQAAN VERSES 7-9	☐ 0.5	☐ 0.5	___ / 1
5	SOORAH AL-FURQAAN VERSES 10-14	☐ 0.5	☐ 0.5	___ / 1
6	SOORAH AL-FURQAAN VERSES 15-16	☐ 0.5	☐ 0.5	___ / 1
7	SOORAH AL-FURQAAN VERSES 17-20 A	☐ 0.5	☐ 0.5	___ / 1
8	SOORAH AL-FURQAAN VERSES 17-20 B	☐ 0.5	☐ 0.5	___ / 1
●	QUIZ 1: LESSONS 1-8 (VERSES 1-20) & MEMORIZATION CHECK			___ / 10
8	SOORAH AL-FURQAAN VERSES 21-23	☐ 0.5	☐ 0.5	___ / 1
10	SOORAH AL-FURQAAN VERSES 24-26	☐ 0.5	☐ 0.5	___ / 1
11	SOORAH AL-FURQAAN VERSES 27-31	☐ 0.5	☐ 0.5	___ / 1
12	SOORAH AL-FURQAAN VERSES 32-33	☐ 0.5	☐ 0.5	___ / 1
13	SOORAH AL-FURQAAN VERSES 34-40	☐ 0.5	☐ 0.5	___ / 1
14	SOORAH AL-FURQAAN VERSES 41-43	☐ 0.5	☐ 0.5	___ / 1
●	QUIZ 2: LESSONS 8-14 (VERSES 21-43) & MEMORIZATION CHECK			___ / 10
15	SOORAH AL-FURQAAN VERSES 44-46	☐ 0.5	☐ 0.5	___ / 1
16	SOORAH AL-FURQAAN VERSES 47-50	☐ 0.5	☐ 0.5	___ / 1
17	SOORAH AL-FURQAAN VERSES 51-55	☐ 0.5	☐ 0.5	___ / 1
18	SOORAH AL-FURQAAN VERSES 56-60	☐ 0.5	☐ 0.5	___ / 1
19	SOORAH AL-FURQAAN VERSES 61-62	☐ 0.5	☐ 0.5	___ / 1
20	SOORAH AL-FURQAAN VERSE 63	☐ 0.5	☐ 0.5	___ / 1
21	SOORAH AL-FURQAAN VERSE 64	☐ 0.5	☐ 0.5	___ / 1
●	QUIZ 3: LESSONS 15-22 (VERSES 44-64) & MEMORIZATION CHECK			___ / 10
22	SOORAH AL-FURQAAN VERSES 65-66	☐ 0.5	☐ 0.5	___ / 1
23	SOORAH AL-FURQAAN VERSE 67	☐ 0.5	☐ 0.5	___ / 1
24	SOORAH AL-FURQAAN VERSES 68-69	☐ 0.5	☐ 0.5	___ / 1
25	SOORAH AL-FURQAAN VERSES 70-71	☐ 0.5	☐ 0.5	___ / 1
26	SOORAH AL-FURQAAN VERSE 72	☐ 0.5	☐ 0.5	___ / 1
27	SOORAH AL-FURQAAN VERSE 73	☐ 0.5	☐ 0.5	___ / 1
28	SOORAH AL-FURQAAN VERSE 74	☐ 0.5	☐ 0.5	___ / 1
●	QUIZ 4: LESSONS 22-28 (VERSES 65-74) & MEMORIZATION CHECK			___ / 10
29	SOORAH AL-FURQAAN VERSES 75-76	☐ 0.5	☐ 0.5	___ / 1
30	SOORAH AL-FURQAAN VERSE 77	☐ 0.5	☐ 0.5	___ / 1
●	QUIZ 5: COMPREHENSIVE FINAL EXAM (VERSES 1-77)			___ / 25
●	COMPREHENSIVE MEMORIZATION CHECK (VERSES 1-77)			___ / 5

TOTAL = _____ %

BEGINNING WITH TOWHEED (THE ONENESS OF ALLAH)

TODAY'S VERSES

قال تعالى: بِسۡمِ ٱللَّهِ ٱلرَّحۡمَٰنِ ٱلرَّحِيمِ

In the Name of Allah, the Most Gracious, the Ever Merciful.

﴿تَبَارَكَ ٱلَّذِى نَزَّلَ ٱلۡفُرۡقَانَ عَلَىٰ عَبۡدِهِۦ لِيَكُونَ لِلۡعَٰلَمِينَ نَذِيرًا ۝ ٱلَّذِى لَهُۥ مُلۡكُ ٱلسَّمَٰوَٰتِ وَٱلۡأَرۡضِ وَلَمۡ يَتَّخِذۡ وَلَدًا وَلَمۡ يَكُن لَّهُۥ شَرِيكٌ فِى ٱلۡمُلۡكِ وَخَلَقَ كُلَّ شَىۡءٍ فَقَدَّرَهُۥ تَقۡدِيرًا ۝﴾

1. Blessed is He Who sent down the Criterion (the Quran) to His worshipful servant, so it would be a warning to the entire creation.

2. [It is] He who possesses the dominion of the heavens and the earth; He has not begotten any son, nor does He have any partner in that dominion. And He created everything and decreed it all with precise measure.

TAFSEER (EXPLANATION) OF THE VERSES

As your teacher reads the *Tafseer* of al-Imam as-Sa'dee (may Allah have Mercy on him), follow along carefully and take notes on the following points:

1. Another name for this *soorah* is:

2. This *soorah* is *Makkiyyah* / *Madaniyyah*. *(Circle one.)*

3. Summarize some differences between *Makkiyyah* and *Madaniyyah* Verses:

MAKKIYYAH	MADANIYYAH

4. Allah's greatness and oneness

5. What does **"tabaaraka"** mean?

6. From the greatest of His blessings:

7. What does *"al-Furqaan"* mean?

8. Who is **"His worshipful servant"**?

9. **"So IT would be a warning…"**

10. The warning of the Quran

11. The results of accepting the warning:

    A. In this life:

    B. In the next life:

    C. What could be a greater blessing!?

12. **"He who possesses the dominion of the heavens and the earth…"**

13. How could He have a son or a partner when this is the reality:

    A. Sovereignty

    B. Power

    C. Sufficiency

    D. Control

14. **"He created everything…"**

15. Everything is decreed in perfect measure.

    87:1-3

    20:50

16. The meanings of the first two Verses lead us to a very important conclusion:

TODAY'S VERSES

قال تعالى:

3. And they have taken gods besides Him; they do not create anything, whilst they are themselves created. They possess no ability to harm nor help their own selves, nor do they possess any ability to cause death, grant life, or resurrect [anyone].

4. Those who disbelieve have said: "This [Quran] is but a lie which he concocted, and others assisted him with that!" Indeed, they come [together] to oppress and conspire in falsehood.

﴿وَٱتَّخَذُواْ مِن دُونِهِۦٓ ءَالِهَةً لَّا يَخْلُقُونَ شَيْئًا وَهُمْ يُخْلَقُونَ وَلَا يَمْلِكُونَ لِأَنفُسِهِمْ ضَرًّا وَلَا نَفْعًا وَلَا يَمْلِكُونَ مَوْتًا وَلَا حَيَوٰةً وَلَا نُشُورًا ٣ وَقَالَ ٱلَّذِينَ كَفَرُوٓاْ إِنْ هَٰذَآ إِلَّآ إِفْكٌ ٱفْتَرَىٰهُ وَأَعَانَهُۥ عَلَيْهِ قَوْمٌ ءَاخَرُونَ فَقَدْ جَآءُو ظُلْمًا وَزُورًا ٤﴾

TAFSEER (EXPLANATION) OF THE VERSES

As your teacher reads the *Tafseer* of al-Imam as-Sa'dee (may Allah have Mercy on him), follow along carefully and take notes on the following points:

1. The most evident proofs of their foolishness and wrongdoing

2. A linguistic benefit about their lack of ability to harm or help

3. Logically, the following conclusions must be made:

    A. About the deities:

    B. About their worshippers:

4. The rightful object of mankind's worship is described with the following things:

1.	5.
2.	6.
3.	7.
4.	8.

5. Stances and consequences:

A.   ➡️

B.   ➡️

6. Two more necessary conclusions:

      A.

      B.

7. They claimed the Quran was a lie.

8. **"Indeed, they come [together] to oppress and conspire in falsehood."**

9. Is it even humanly possible to fake the Quran?

10. Did the Prophet conspire with anyone?

MYTHS OF THE ANCIENTS OR DIVINE REVELATION?

TODAY'S VERSES

5. And they have said, "Myths of the ancients is what he has copied down, as they are dictated to him morning and night."

6. Say: The One who sent it down is He who knows the secrets within the heavens and earth. He is and has always been Oft-Forgiving, Ever Merciful.

قال تعالى:

﴿وَقَالُوٓاْ أَسَٰطِيرُ ٱلۡأَوَّلِينَ ٱكۡتَتَبَهَا فَهِىَ تُمۡلَىٰ عَلَيۡهِ بُكۡرَةً وَأَصِيلٗا ۝ قُلۡ أَنزَلَهُ ٱلَّذِى يَعۡلَمُ ٱلسِّرَّ فِى ٱلسَّمَٰوَٰتِ وَٱلۡأَرۡضِۚ إِنَّهُۥ كَانَ غَفُورٗا رَّحِيمٗا ۝﴾

TAFSEER (EXPLANATION) OF THE VERSES

As your teacher reads the *Tafseer* of al-Imam as-Sa'dee (may Allah have Mercy on him), follow along carefully and take notes on the following points:

1. Another one of their claims

2. **"Myths of the ancients..."**

3. They claim he merely copied down tales that were dictated to him.

4. This poorly thought-out accusation actually includes:

   A. About the Prophet:

   B. About the Quran:

   C. About themselves:

   D. An illiterate man is now writing things!?

5. Allah knows the secrets within the heavens and earth.

6. A similar affirmation [26:192-194]

7. The angle of refutation in this description of Allah

8. The conclusion: If you are really going to claim this, then:

9. A subtle benefit about mentioning Allah's Knowledge

10. The result of contemplating the Quran:

11. Despite their disbelief, Allah's Grace is still extended to them:

12. An invitation to Allah's Forgiveness

13. Reflecting over many angles of Allah's Mercy upon them:

     A.

     B.

     C.

     D.

     E.

DISBELIEVERS INSIST ON THEIR BASELESS ASSUMPTIONS

TODAY'S VERSES

قال تعالى:

7. And they have said, "What is with this messenger, eating food and walking in the marketplaces? Had there only been an angel sent down to him, to be a warner along with him."

8. "Or had treasure been given to him, or if he had a garden from which he could eat." The [most] oppressive ones said, "You follow but a man under the influence of magic."

9. Look at the likenesses they have put forth to describe you, [as a result] they have gone astray, and they are not able to find a way back.

﴿وَقَالُوا۟ مَالِ هَٰذَا ٱلرَّسُولِ يَأْكُلُ ٱلطَّعَامَ وَيَمْشِى فِى ٱلْأَسْوَاقِ لَوْلَآ أُنزِلَ إِلَيْهِ مَلَكٌ فَيَكُونَ مَعَهُۥ نَذِيرًا ۝ أَوْ يُلْقَىٰٓ إِلَيْهِ كَنزٌ أَوْ تَكُونُ لَهُۥ جَنَّةٌ يَأْكُلُ مِنْهَا۟ وَقَالَ ٱلظَّٰلِمُونَ إِن تَتَّبِعُونَ إِلَّا رَجُلًا مَّسْحُورًا ۝ ٱنظُرْ كَيْفَ ضَرَبُوا۟ لَكَ ٱلْأَمْثَٰلَ فَضَلُّوا۟ فَلَا يَسْتَطِيعُونَ سَبِيلًا ۝﴾

TAFSEER (EXPLANATION) OF THE VERSES

As your teacher reads the *Tafseer* of al-Imam as-Sa'dee (may Allah have Mercy on him), follow along carefully and take notes on the following points:

1. Who is being quoted?

2. What do they insist a messenger should be?

3. **"What is with this messenger…?"**

4. Their problem with his consumption of food

5. Their problem with him walking in the markets

6. Previewing Verse 20 of *Soorah al-Furqaan*:

7. They insist that an angel should come down to openly support him.

8. A human being alone is not enough, as they insist.

9. **"Or had treasure been given to him…"**

10. **"Or if he had a garden from which he could eat…"**

11. At the root of these points

12. Claiming he was a man under the influence of magic

13. The absurdity of these claims, summarized in a brief comment

14. A summary of their claims:

      A.

      B.

      C.

      D.

      E.

15. The result: **"They have gone astray…"**

16. A simple moment of reflection about these claims

17. The divine command to consider and contemplate the claims

18. Allah had what is better in store for His Messenger

TODAY'S VERSES

10. Blessed is He who, if He so wills, shall grant you what is better than that: gardens under which rivers flow, and He shall make palaces for you [in Paradise].

11. Yet, they reject [belief in] the Hour (the Day of Judgment). And We have prepared for those who reject the Hour a blazing fire.

12. When it (Hell) sees them from far away, they hear its furious rage and roar.

13. And when they are thrown into a crowded place within it, chained together, they wail in agony therein.

14. Do not wail in agony only once on this day, but wail in agony many times over!

قال تعالى:

﴿تَبَارَكَ ٱلَّذِى إِن شَآءَ جَعَلَ لَكَ خَيْرًا مِّن ذَٰلِكَ جَنَّٰتٍ تَجْرِى مِن تَحْتِهَا ٱلْأَنْهَٰرُ وَيَجْعَل لَّكَ قُصُورًا ۝ بَلْ كَذَّبُوا۟ بِٱلسَّاعَةِ ۖ وَأَعْتَدْنَا لِمَن كَذَّبَ بِٱلسَّاعَةِ سَعِيرًا ۝ إِذَا رَأَتْهُم مِّن مَّكَانٍ بَعِيدٍ سَمِعُوا۟ لَهَا تَغَيُّظًا وَزَفِيرًا ۝ وَإِذَآ أُلْقُوا۟ مِنْهَا مَكَانًا ضَيِّقًا مُّقَرَّنِينَ دَعَوْا۟ هُنَالِكَ ثُبُورًا ۝ لَّا تَدْعُوا۟ ٱلْيَوْمَ ثُبُورًا وَٰحِدًا وَٱدْعُوا۟ ثُبُورًا كَثِيرًا ۝﴾

TAFSEER (EXPLANATION) OF THE VERSES

As your teacher reads the *Tafseer* of al-Imam as-Sa'dee (may Allah have Mercy on him), follow along carefully and take notes on the following points:

1. A brief summary of the misguided claims of the disbelievers

2. Palaces in Paradise

3. Allah's Power and Capability

4. The reality of worldly enjoyment and material possessions

5. Insisting that revelation come with great wealth

6. A divine exposition of the basis of their objections

7. They reject belief in the Hour.

8. The only resolution for arrogant denial of the truth

9. The Hellfire described as *"Sa'eer"*

10. **"When it sees them from far away..."**

11. The effects of hearing the Hellfire's rage and roar from afar:

     A.

     B.

     C.

     D.

12. Their situation in the Hellfire:

     A.

     B.

     C.

13. When and where do they call out in agony?

14. What is *"thuboor"*?

15. They will acknowledge their own wickedness and wrongdoing.

16. Their wails of agony provide no relief.

17. **"But wail in agony many times over!"**

18. The relationship of the next Verses and topics

THE CHOICE IS YOURS: WHICH OUTCOME IS BETTER?

TODAY'S VERSES

15. Say: Is that [torment] better or the Garden of Eternity promised to the pious? It will be theirs as a reward and a final destination.

16. They shall have therein all they desire, abiding therein forever. That is a promise from your Lord, sought from Him [alone].

قال تعالى:

﴿قُل أَذَٰلِكَ خَيْرٌ أَمْ جَنَّةُ ٱلْخُلْدِ ٱلَّتِى وُعِدَ ٱلْمُتَّقُونَ كَانَتْ لَهُمْ جَزَآءً وَمَصِيرًا ۝ لَّهُمْ فِيهَا مَا يَشَآءُونَ خَٰلِدِينَ كَانَ عَلَىٰ رَبِّكَ وَعْدًا مَّسْـُٔولًا ۝﴾

TAFSEER (EXPLANATION) OF THE VERSES

As your teacher reads the *Tafseer* of al-Imam as-Sa'dee (may Allah have Mercy on him), follow along carefully and take notes on the following points:

1. The point of this command to tell them this

2. **"Is <u>that</u> better...?"**

3. The garden promised to the pious

4. A reward/recompense

5. A final destination

6. "They shall have therein all they desire..."

7. "__IT__ will be theirs..."

8. Something sought from Him, in two ways:

| | |
| | |

9. Which of the two abodes is better?

   And which of the two types of people are better?

10. Truth is clarified; excuses are cut off.

11. The author supplicates for himself and the readers:

فَنَرْجُوكَ يَا مَنْ قَضَيْتَ عَلَى أَقْوَامٍ بِالشَّقَاءِ وَأَقْوَامٍ بِالسَّعَادَةِ: أَنْ تَجْعَلَنَا مِمَّنْ كَتَبْتَ لَهُمُ الحُسْنَى وَزِيَادَةً، وَنَسْتَغِيثُ بِكَ اللَّهُمَّ مِنْ حَالَةِ الأَشْقِيَاءِ، وَنَسْأَلُكَ المُعَافَاةَ مِنْهَا!

12. A reminder about a neglected _Sunnah_ [not from the _Tafseer_ of al-Imam as-Sa'dee]

DISGRACED & DISPROVEN IN THE HELLFIRE (PART ONE)

TODAY'S VERSES

17. On the day when He gathers them along with what they worship besides Allah, and He says: "Was it you who misled these servants of Mine, or did they go astray from the path [on their own]?"

18. They say, "Exalted You are! It was not for us to take any protecting allies besides You, but You gave them and their fathers comfort until they forgot the reminder and became people who were ruined."

19. They have shown you to be liars for what you have said; now you have no ability to deflect [punishment away from yourselves] or to get any help. And whoever of you oppresses, We shall make him taste a severe punishment.

20. And We sent no messengers before you except that they actually ate food and walked in marketplaces. And We have made some of you as trials for others, so will you have patience? And your Lord is All–Seeing.

قال تعالى:

﴿وَيَوْمَ يَحْشُرُهُمْ وَمَا يَعْبُدُونَ مِن دُونِ ٱللَّهِ فَيَقُولُ ءَأَنتُمْ أَضْلَلْتُمْ عِبَادِى هَٰؤُلَآءِ أَمْ هُمْ ضَلُّوا۟ ٱلسَّبِيلَ ۝ قَالُوا۟ سُبْحَٰنَكَ مَا كَانَ يَنۢبَغِى لَنَآ أَن نَّتَّخِذَ مِن دُونِكَ مِنْ أَوْلِيَآءَ وَلَٰكِن مَّتَّعْتَهُمْ وَءَابَآءَهُمْ حَتَّىٰ نَسُوا۟ ٱلذِّكْرَ وَكَانُوا۟ قَوْمًۢا بُورًا ۝ فَقَدْ كَذَّبُوكُم بِمَا تَقُولُونَ فَمَا تَسْتَطِيعُونَ صَرْفًا وَلَا نَصْرًا وَمَن يَظْلِم مِّنكُمْ نُذِقْهُ عَذَابًا كَبِيرًا ۝ وَمَآ أَرْسَلْنَا قَبْلَكَ مِنَ ٱلْمُرْسَلِينَ إِلَّآ إِنَّهُمْ لَيَأْكُلُونَ ٱلطَّعَامَ وَيَمْشُونَ فِى ٱلْأَسْوَاقِ وَجَعَلْنَا بَعْضَكُمْ لِبَعْضٍ فِتْنَةً أَتَصْبِرُونَ وَكَانَ رَبُّكَ بَصِيرًا ۝﴾

TAFSEER (EXPLANATION) OF THE VERSES

As your teacher reads the *Tafseer* of al-Imam as-Sa'dee (may Allah have Mercy on him), follow along carefully and take notes on the following points:

1. The situation of the disbelievers on the Day of Judgment

2. **"When He gathers <u>them</u>…"**

3. **"And <u>He</u> says…"** (to whom?)

4. **"Did you mislead these servants of Mine, or did they go astray on their own?"**

5. Their exaltation serves two basic purposes:

6. The helpless & incapable cannot possibly think to ask others to worship them!

7. Similar statements on the Day of Judgment

    A. From 'Eesaa (Jesus): [5:116-117]

    B. From the angels: [34:40-41]

    C. From the people: [46:6]

8. The real reason for their misguidance

9. **"Until they forgot the reminder…"**

10. The meaning of the word *"boor"*

11. No goodness within them, along with their enjoyment of worldly pleasures

12. The worshippers are declared liars.

13. All three claims rejected and disproven:

14. Objects of worship are now enemies to their worshippers!

15. Incapable of *"sarf"*

16. Incapable of *"nasr"*

17. Such is the fate of the ignorant blind-followers among the disbelievers.

18. So then what about those who knew better…? *(The study of these Verses continues in tomorrow's lesson, in shaa' Allah…)*

YESTERDAY'S VERSES (AGAIN)

17. On the day when He gathers them along with what they worship besides Allah, and He says: "Was it you who misled these servants of Mine, or did they go astray from the path [on their own]?"

18. They say, "Exalted You are! It was not for us to take any protecting allies besides You, but You gave them and their fathers comfort until they forgot the reminder and became people who were ruined."

19. They have shown you to be liars for what you have said; now you have no ability to deflect [punishment away from yourselves] or to get any help. And whoever of you oppresses, We shall make him taste a severe punishment.

20. And We sent no messengers before you except that they actually ate food and walked in marketplaces. And We have made some of you as trials for others, so will you have patience? And your Lord is All-Seeing.

قال تعالى:

﴿وَيَوْمَ يَحْشُرُهُمْ وَمَا يَعْبُدُونَ مِن دُونِ ٱللَّهِ فَيَقُولُ ءَأَنتُمْ أَضْلَلْتُمْ عِبَادِى هَـٰٓؤُلَآءِ أَمْ هُمْ ضَلُّواْ ٱلسَّبِيلَ ۞ قَالُواْ سُبْحَـٰنَكَ مَا كَانَ يَنۢبَغِى لَنَآ أَن نَّتَّخِذَ مِن دُونِكَ مِنْ أَوْلِيَآءَ وَلَـٰكِن مَّتَّعْتَهُمْ وَءَابَآءَهُمْ حَتَّىٰ نَسُواْ ٱلذِّكْرَ وَكَانُواْ قَوْمًۢا بُورًا ۞ فَقَدْ كَذَّبُوكُم بِمَا تَقُولُونَ فَمَا تَسْتَطِيعُونَ صَرْفًا وَلَا نَصْرًا ۞ وَمَن يَظْلِم مِّنكُمْ نُذِقْهُ عَذَابًا كَبِيرًا ۞ وَمَآ أَرْسَلْنَا قَبْلَكَ مِنَ ٱلْمُرْسَلِينَ إِلَّآ إِنَّهُمْ لَيَأْكُلُونَ ٱلطَّعَامَ وَيَمْشُونَ فِى ٱلْأَسْوَاقِ وَجَعَلْنَا بَعْضَكُمْ لِبَعْضٍ فِتْنَةً أَتَصْبِرُونَ وَكَانَ رَبُّكَ بَصِيرًا ۞﴾

TAFSEER (EXPLANATION) OF THE VERSES

As your teacher continues reading the *Tafseer* of al-Imam as-Sa'dee (may Allah have Mercy on him), follow along carefully and take notes on the following points:

18. From yesterday's lesson: What about the fate of those who knew better?

19. What kind of *"thulm"*?

20. **"We shall make him taste a severe punishment."**

21. **Verse 20** is a response to their objection mentioned in **Verse 7**:

22. Humans, not angels, like the previous messengers

23. From Allah's Wisdom: Wealth shall be a trial.

24. How are some people trials for others?

       A.

       B.

       C.

       D.

       E.

25. The overall goal and wisdom of such trials:

26. Two potential outcomes:

27. **"And your Lord is All-Seeing."**

       A.

       B.

       C.

       D.

       E.

THE DAY THE DISBELIEVERS WILL SEE THE ANGELS

TODAY'S VERSES

21. And those who do not long for the meeting with Us (i.e., disbelievers in the Day of Judgment) have said, "Had only the angels been sent down to us, or we could see our Lord!" They indeed have arrogance in their souls; they have transgressed with terrible transgressions.

22. On the day they see the angels, no glad tidings on such a day for the criminals. They (the angels) say, "Not allowed; denied!"

23. And We turn to whatever deeds they did, and We make that into scattered dust.

قال تعالى:

﴿وَقَالَ ٱلَّذِينَ لَا يَرْجُونَ لِقَآءَنَا لَوْلَآ أُنزِلَ عَلَيْنَا ٱلْمَلَـٰٓئِكَةُ أَوْ نَرَىٰ رَبَّنَا لَقَدِ ٱسْتَكْبَرُواْ فِىٓ أَنفُسِهِمْ وَعَتَوْ عُتُوًّا كَبِيرًا ۞ يَوْمَ يَرَوْنَ ٱلْمَلَـٰٓئِكَةَ لَا بُشْرَىٰ يَوْمَئِذٍ لِّلْمُجْرِمِينَ وَيَقُولُونَ حِجْرًا مَّحْجُورًا ۞ وَقَدِمْنَآ إِلَىٰ مَا عَمِلُواْ مِنْ عَمَلٍ فَجَعَلْنَـٰهُ هَبَآءً مَّنثُورًا ۞﴾

TAFSEER (EXPLANATION) OF THE VERSES

As your teacher reads the *Tafseer* of al-Imam as-Sa'dee (may Allah have Mercy on him), follow along carefully and take notes on the following points:

1. Who are **"those who do not long for the meeting with Us"**?

2. Their demand to have the angels come down

3. Their demand to see Allah

4. The reality of this opposition to the Messenger

5. **"They indeed have arrogance in their souls…"**

6. A complete lack of self-awareness

7. The result of this arrogance and transgression

8. No admonition or reminder has any effect

9. The punishment for them, from three ways:

10. They see the angels (They asked for it!)

11. **"No glad tidings on such a day for the criminals..."**

12. Seeing angels at the time of death

    [6:93]

13. Seeing angels in the grave

14. Angels pushing them towards Hell on the Day of Judgment

15. Angels are caretakers of the Hellfire

16. When they finally get what they asked for....

17. **"They (the angels) say, 'Not allowed; denied!'"**

    [55:33]

    [From the *Tafseer* of al-Imam al-Baghawi]

        Ibn 'Abbaas:

        Muqaatil:

        Others:

        Ibn Jurayj:

18. **"And We turn to whatever deeds they did..."**

19. Real deeds changed into scattered dust

20. What is the cause of this situation?

21. Which deeds will NOT be made into scattered dust on that day?

TODAY'S VERSES

24. The residents of Paradise on that day have better abodes and finer places of relaxation.

25. The day when the sky cracks apart with clouds, and the angels are made to descend, an undeniably real descending.

26. All sovereignty on that day is rightfully owned by the Most Gracious (Allah alone); for the disbelievers it is a day of difficulty.

قال تعالى:

﴿أَصۡحَٰبُ ٱلۡجَنَّةِ يَوۡمَئِذٍ خَيۡرٌ مُّسۡتَقَرًّا وَأَحۡسَنُ مَقِيلًا ٢٤ وَيَوۡمَ تَشَقَّقُ ٱلسَّمَآءُ بِٱلۡغَمَٰمِ وَنُزِّلَ ٱلۡمَلَٰٓئِكَةُ تَنزِيلًا ٢٥ ٱلۡمُلۡكُ يَوۡمَئِذٍ ٱلۡحَقُّ لِلرَّحۡمَٰنِ وَكَانَ يَوۡمًا عَلَى ٱلۡكَٰفِرِينَ عَسِيرًا ٢٦﴾

TAFSEER (EXPLANATION) OF THE VERSES

As your teacher reads the *Tafseer* of al-Imam as-Sa'dee (may Allah have Mercy on him), follow along carefully and take notes on the following points:

1. When is this day?

2. Who are the residents of Paradise?

3. Better and finer – than what?

4. What is a *"maqeel"*?

5. The better abode and finer place of relaxation

6. Comparatively, the Hellfire is:

> [Preview: Verse 66 of *Soorah al-Furqaan*]

7. A general benefit about comparisons in the Quran

> 27:59
>
> [Preview: Verse 34 of *Soorah al-Furqaan*]
>
> 3:110
>
> 62:9

8. Terrifying descriptions of the Day of Judgment

9. The clouds and the descending of the angels

    A.

    B.

10. The humble servitude of the angels

11. **"For the disbelievers it is a day of difficulty."**

    19:85

    19:86

12. **"All sovereignty on <u>that</u> day…"**

13. Power, influence, authority, etc. removed

14. Indications from the name used: *ar-Rahmaan**

*After studying al-Imam as-Sa'dee's explanation of the 14th point, consider:

    A. The insight of this scholar (all of this from a single word)
    B. The power of a single word in the Quran
    C. The detailed meanings within Allah's Names and Attributes
    D. The importance of reflecting over the Quran

TODAY'S VERSES

27. The day when the wrongdoer bites at his hands, saying, "I wish I would have taken a path following along with the Messenger!"

28. "O woe to me! I wish I had never taken So-and-So as a close friend!"

29. "He did indeed lead me astray from the Reminder (the Quran) after it had come to me." The devil continues to betray and desert people.

30. And the Messenger says: "O my Lord! My people have indeed abandoned this Quran."

31. Thus We assign to every prophet an enemy among the criminals, whilst your Lord suffices as a Guide and a Helper.

قال تعالى:

﴿وَيَوْمَ يَعَضُّ ٱلظَّالِمُ عَلَىٰ يَدَيْهِ يَقُولُ يَٰلَيْتَنِي ٱتَّخَذْتُ مَعَ ٱلرَّسُولِ سَبِيلًا ۝ يَٰوَيْلَتَىٰ لَيْتَنِي لَمْ أَتَّخِذْ فُلَانًا خَلِيلًا ۝ لَّقَدْ أَضَلَّنِي عَنِ ٱلذِّكْرِ بَعْدَ إِذْ جَآءَنِي ۗ وَكَانَ ٱلشَّيْطَٰنُ لِلْإِنسَٰنِ خَذُولًا ۝ وَقَالَ ٱلرَّسُولُ يَٰرَبِّ إِنَّ قَوْمِي ٱتَّخَذُوا۟ هَٰذَا ٱلْقُرْءَانَ مَهْجُورًا ۝ وَكَذَٰلِكَ جَعَلْنَا لِكُلِّ نَبِيٍّ عَدُوًّا مِّنَ ٱلْمُجْرِمِينَ ۗ وَكَفَىٰ بِرَبِّكَ هَادِيًا وَنَصِيرًا ۝﴾

TAFSEER (EXPLANATION) OF THE VERSES

As your teacher reads the *Tafseer* of al-Imam as-Sa'dee (may Allah have Mercy on him), follow along carefully and take notes on the following points:

1. Who is this **"wrongdoer"**?

2. What is the meaning of biting at his hands?

3. His declaration of regret

4. Who was **"So-and-So"**?

5. What is a *"khaleel"*?

6. Realization: Who did I reject and hate?

   Who did I take as an ally?

7. How does the devil lead people astray?

8. The devil's step-by-step process of betrayal:

	→		→		→	

9. The devil addresses his followers on the Day of Judgment:

> 14:22

10. Based on this, consider these three important pieces of advice:

11. **"And the Messenger says…"**

12. **"O my Lord! My people…"**

13. Abandoning the Quran

14. The required manners with the Quran:

15. **"Thus We assign to every prophet an enemy among the criminals…"**

16. What kind of people are these designated enemies?

17. What do they do?

18. The worldly benefit of this opposition

19. The wisdom of this opposition relative to the Hereafter

20. Allah's Guidance is sufficient.

21. Allah's Aid is sufficient.

22. The course of action indicated in the closing of the Verse:

TODAY'S VERSES

32. And those who disbelieve have said: "Had only the Quran been sent down to him all at once!" Like that [it was revealed in stages], so We would make your heart firm with it. And We have revealed it gradually, in stages.

33. And they bring you no parable except that We bring you the Truth [about that matter] and a better explanation of it.

قال تعالى:

﴿وَقَالَ ٱلَّذِينَ كَفَرُواْ لَوْلَا نُزِّلَ عَلَيْهِ ٱلْقُرْءَانُ جُمْلَةً وَٰحِدَةً كَذَٰلِكَ لِنُثَبِّتَ بِهِۦ فُؤَادَكَ وَرَتَّلْنَٰهُ تَرْتِيلًا ۝ وَلَا يَأْتُونَكَ بِمَثَلٍ إِلَّا جِئْنَٰكَ بِٱلْحَقِّ وَأَحْسَنَ تَفْسِيرًا ۝﴾

TAFSEER (EXPLANATION) OF THE VERSES

As your teacher reads the *Tafseer* of al-Imam as-Sa'dee (may Allah have Mercy on him), follow along carefully and take notes on the following points:

1. Another demand of the disbelievers

2. The basis of their demand

3. And what is the real problem in revealing it in stages?

4. **"So We would make your heart firm with it…"**

5. Exploring one aspect of how revelation in stages was more appropriate:

6. **"And We have revealed it gradually, in stages."**

7. Special attention to this matter

8. **"And they bring you no parable…"**

9. The Truth and a better explanation:

MEANINGS:	➡	
WORDINGS:	➡	

10. Teachers and preachers can adopt this Quranic mannerism

11. A refutation of the Jahmiyyah and other deviants

TODAY'S VERSES

قال تعالى:

34. Those gathered upon their faces unto Jahannam, such are in a worse place, [upon] a more misguided path.

35. And indeed We gave Moosaa (Moses) the Book and appointed his brother, Haaroon (Aaron), as a helper for him.

36. And We said: "Go to the people who have disbelieved in Our aayaat (signs and verses)." Then, We destroyed them with utter destruction.

37. And Nooh's (Noah's) people, when they disbelieved in the messengers, We drowned them; We made them a lesson of guidance for all humankind. And We have prepared a painful punishment for the wrong doers.

38. And [the civilizations of] 'Aad and Thamood, as well as the people of [the Well of] Ar–Rass, including many generations between those.

39. For each [of them] We provided examples [to guide them], yet each [of them] We annihilated with absolute destruction.

40. And indeed they have come to the town which had evil rain poured down upon it. Did they not even see it [themselves, firsthand]? Yet they [still] would not hope for any resurrection.

ٱلَّذِينَ يُحْشَرُونَ عَلَىٰ وُجُوهِهِمْ إِلَىٰ جَهَنَّمَ أُوْلَـٰٓئِكَ شَرٌّ مَّكَانًا وَأَضَلُّ سَبِيلًا ۝ وَلَقَدْ ءَاتَيْنَا مُوسَى ٱلْكِتَـٰبَ وَجَعَلْنَا مَعَهُۥٓ أَخَاهُ هَـٰرُونَ وَزِيرًا ۝ فَقُلْنَا ٱذْهَبَآ إِلَى ٱلْقَوْمِ ٱلَّذِينَ كَذَّبُوا۟ بِـَٔايَـٰتِنَا فَدَمَّرْنَـٰهُمْ تَدْمِيرًا ۝ وَقَوْمَ نُوحٍ لَّمَّا كَذَّبُوا۟ ٱلرُّسُلَ أَغْرَقْنَـٰهُمْ وَجَعَلْنَـٰهُمْ لِلنَّاسِ ءَايَةً وَأَعْتَدْنَا لِلظَّـٰلِمِينَ عَذَابًا أَلِيمًا ۝ وَعَادًا وَثَمُودَا۟ وَأَصْحَـٰبَ ٱلرَّسِّ وَقُرُونًۢا بَيْنَ ذَٰلِكَ كَثِيرًا ۝ وَكُلًّا ضَرَبْنَا لَهُ ٱلْأَمْثَـٰلَ وَكُلًّا تَبَّرْنَا تَتْبِيرًا ۝ وَلَقَدْ أَتَوْا۟ عَلَى ٱلْقَرْيَةِ ٱلَّتِىٓ أُمْطِرَتْ مَطَرَ ٱلسَّوْءِ أَفَلَمْ يَكُونُوا۟ يَرَوْنَهَا بَلْ كَانُوا۟ لَا يَرْجُونَ نُشُورًا ۝

TAFSEER (EXPLANATION) OF THE VERSES

As your teacher reads the *Tafseer* of al-Imam as-Sa'dee (may Allah have Mercy on him), follow along carefully and take notes on the following points:

1. Who is being treated this way?

2. The reality of this treatment

3. Where are they being taken?

4. **"Such [people]…"**

5. **"In a worse place…"** (comparatively)

6. A reminder about comparing "incomparable" situations.

   Review: Lesson 10, point 7

7. The point of mentioning these examples of the nations of the past

8. Some of those civilizations have visible relics.

   54:43

9. **"Yet they [still] would not hope for any resurrection."**

10. They had *aayaat* (signs and Verses) come to them as well.

MOCKING THE TRUTH YET STUBBORN UPON FALSEHOOD

TODAY'S VERSES

41. And when they see you, they only take you as a joke, [saying]: "Is this the one whom Allah has sent as a Messenger?"

42. "He would have nearly misled us away from our gods, had it not been that we were steadfast [in our worship of them]!" And they will come to know when they see the punishment, who is most misguided!

43. Have you seen him who has taken his own whims as his god? Could you then be responsible for him?

قال تعالى:

﴿وَإِذَا رَأَوۡكَ إِن يَتَّخِذُونَكَ إِلَّا هُزُوًا أَهَٰذَا ٱلَّذِى بَعَثَ ٱللَّهُ رَسُولًا ۝ إِن كَادَ لَيُضِلُّنَا عَنۡ ءَالِهَتِنَا لَوۡلَآ أَن صَبَرۡنَا عَلَيۡهَاۚ وَسَوۡفَ يَعۡلَمُونَ حِينَ يَرَوۡنَ ٱلۡعَذَابَ مَنۡ أَضَلُّ سَبِيلًا ۝ أَرَءَيۡتَ مَنِ ٱتَّخَذَ إِلَٰهَهُۥ هَوَىٰهُ أَفَأَنتَ تَكُونُ عَلَيۡهِ وَكِيلًا ۝﴾

TAFSEER (EXPLANATION) OF THE VERSES

As your teacher reads the *Tafseer* of al-Imam as-Sa'dee (may Allah have Mercy on him), follow along carefully and take notes on the following points:

1. **"And when <u>they</u> see you..."**

2. What do they do?

3. What do they say?

4. Their rancor against the Prophet

5. This resembles another Verse:

> 43:32

6. Their reality, based on this kind of speech

7. The reality of the Prophet (صلى الله عليه وسلم)

8. While his mockers are known to embody the following traits:

9. From their mockery and slander:

10. Who do they claim might have misled them?

11. What do they mean by misleading them away from their gods?

12. Being patient on what kind of situation?

13. A similar Verse: [38:6]

14. When is patience not a virtue?

15. The patience of the believers:

      103:3

16. Since this is what they choose to remain patient upon

17. **"And they will come to know when they see the punishment, who is most misguided"**

18. Recognition, regret, and remorse mentioned previously

      Review: Verses 27-29

19. The taking of desires as a god

20. The peculiar audacity of such a person

21. You are not responsible for such people.

TODAY'S VERSES

قال تعالى:

44. Or do you assume that most of them [actually] listen or comprehend? They are only like cattle, or yet even further astray [than cattle]!

45. Have you not seen how your Lord extends the shadow? Had He willed, He would have made it still. Then, We have made the sun its guide.

46. Then, We bring it back unto Us in gradual withdrawal.

﴿أَمْ تَحْسَبُ أَنَّ أَكْثَرَهُمْ يَسْمَعُونَ أَوْ يَعْقِلُونَ إِنْ هُمْ إِلَّا كَالْأَنْعَامِ بَلْ هُمْ أَضَلُّ سَبِيلًا ۝ أَلَمْ تَرَ إِلَىٰ رَبِّكَ كَيْفَ مَدَّ الظِّلَّ وَلَوْ شَاءَ لَجَعَلَهُ سَاكِنًا ثُمَّ جَعَلْنَا الشَّمْسَ عَلَيْهِ دَلِيلًا ۝ ثُمَّ قَبَضْنَاهُ إِلَيْنَا قَبْضًا يَسِيرًا ۝﴾

TAFSEER (EXPLANATION) OF THE VERSES

As your teacher reads the *Tafseer* of al-Imam as-Sa'dee (may Allah have Mercy on him), follow along carefully and take notes on the following points:

1. The likeness of the disbelievers

    2:171

2. How are cattle more rightly guided?

    A.

    B.

    C.

3. The resulting conclusion:

4. **"Have you not seen...?"**

5. What does it prove about Allah?

6. When is this phenomenon?

7. Making the sun <u>its</u> guide

8. How would we have shade without the sun?

9. **"Then, We bring it back unto Us in gradual withdrawal."**

10. Benefits of considering this phenomenon

FROM THE MANY FAVORS AND BLESSINGS OF ALLAH

TODAY'S VERSES

قال تعالى:

47. And He is the One who has made the night a covering for you and sleep as relaxation, and He has made the daytime [for you to] spread out.

48. And He is the One who has sent the winds as favorable signs of His imminent Mercy (i.e., the rain). And We have sent down clean [and purifying] water from the sky;

49. So that We give life by it to dead land, and We provide drink from it to what We have created of cattle and so many people.

50. And indeed We have distributed it amongst them so they might be reminded, but most people refuse to be anything but ingrates.

﴿وَهُوَ ٱلَّذِى جَعَلَ لَكُمُ ٱلَّيْلَ لِبَاسًا وَٱلنَّوْمَ سُبَاتًا وَجَعَلَ ٱلنَّهَارَ نُشُورًا ۝ وَهُوَ ٱلَّذِىٓ أَرْسَلَ ٱلرِّيَـٰحَ بُشْرًۢا بَيْنَ يَدَىْ رَحْمَتِهِۦ وَأَنزَلْنَا مِنَ ٱلسَّمَآءِ مَآءً طَهُورًا ۝ لِّنُحْـِۦىَ بِهِۦ بَلْدَةً مَّيْتًا وَنُسْقِيَهُۥ مِمَّا خَلَقْنَآ أَنْعَـٰمًا وَأَنَاسِىَّ كَثِيرًا ۝ وَلَقَدْ صَرَّفْنَـٰهُ بَيْنَهُمْ لِيَذَّكَّرُوا۟ فَأَبَىٰٓ أَكْثَرُ ٱلنَّاسِ إِلَّا كُفُورًا ۝﴾

TAFSEER (EXPLANATION) OF THE VERSES

As your teacher reads the *Tafseer* of al-Imam as-Sa'dee (may Allah have Mercy on him), follow along carefully and take notes on the following points:

1. From the Kindness and Mercy of Allah

2. The meaning of the word, *"subaat"*

3. What would happen...?

    Harms of continual daytime:

    Harms of unending night:

4. The daytime is for "spreading out".

*REVIEW: *Soorah an-Naba'* (78:9-11)

5. "And He is the One who has sent the winds..."

6. Winds as signs of Mercy

7. The meaning of *"tahoor"*

8. The blessing of life given to dead ground

9. Water for people and animals

10. Reflection: About the One who sends the winds & rain

11. Those who fail to receive this reminder

BLESSINGS IN THE ENVIRONMENT & WITHIN FAMILY

TODAY'S VERSES

قال تعالى:

51. And had We so willed, We would have sent a warner to every town.

52. So do not obey the disbelievers; instead engage them with it (the Quran), with great efforts [in propagating Islam].

53. And He is the One who has released both bodies of water; this one is sweet and palatable, and the other is salty and bitter. And He has made a barrier and a fortified partition between them.

54. And He is the One who created humankind from water, and He has made relatives for him through blood lineage and marriage. And your Lord is All-Capable.

55. And yet they worship others besides Allah, things which cannot help them nor harm them! The disbeliever is ever supportive [of falsehood] in opposition to your Lord.

﴿وَلَوْ شِئْنَا لَبَعَثْنَا فِي كُلِّ قَرْيَةٍ نَّذِيرًا ۝ فَلَا تُطِعِ ٱلْكَٰفِرِينَ وَجَٰهِدْهُم بِهِۦ جِهَادًا كَبِيرًا ۝ وَهُوَ ٱلَّذِى مَرَجَ ٱلْبَحْرَيْنِ هَٰذَا عَذْبٌ فُرَاتٌ وَهَٰذَا مِلْحٌ أُجَاجٌ وَجَعَلَ بَيْنَهُمَا بَرْزَخًا وَحِجْرًا مَّحْجُورًا ۝ وَهُوَ ٱلَّذِى خَلَقَ مِنَ ٱلْمَآءِ بَشَرًا فَجَعَلَهُۥ نَسَبًا وَصِهْرًا وَكَانَ رَبُّكَ قَدِيرًا ۝ وَيَعْبُدُونَ مِن دُونِ ٱللَّهِ مَا لَا يَنفَعُهُمْ وَلَا يَضُرُّهُمْ وَكَانَ ٱلْكَافِرُ عَلَىٰ رَبِّهِۦ ظَهِيرًا ۝

TAFSEER (EXPLANATION) OF THE VERSES

As your teacher reads the *Tafseer* of al-Imam as-Sa'dee (may Allah have Mercy on him), follow along carefully and take notes on the following points:

1. Allah's unrestricted *"mashee'ah"*

2. The meaning of *"natheer"*

3. His Will coincides with His Wisdom

4. No obedience to the disbelievers

5. Prohibitions include orders of their opposites.

6. **"Engage them with it..."**

7. Engage them with a great kind of *jihaad*, which includes:

      A.

      B.

      C.

      D.

> ***BENEFIT:** *Jihaad* ordered in a Makkan *soorah*, what does it prove?

8. **"And He is the One who has released both bodies of water…"**

9. The two kinds of water:

	➡
	➡

10. The ***"barzakh"*** between them

    [55:19-20]

11. The ***"hijr mahjoor"*** between them

12. **"And He is the One who created humankind from water…"**

13. He then spread them all over earth

14. A testimony to His Power

15. Which proves an especially important point:

16. **"And yet they worship… things which cannot help them nor harm them!"**

17. The obligation they were supposed to uphold

18. Disbelievers support falsehood over the truth.

19. Despite how many blessings from Allah they have enjoyed

20. Allah still bestows blessings upon them, despite their ingratitude.

TODAY'S VERSES

56. And We have only sent you as a herald of glad tidings and a warner.

57. Say: I do not ask you for any compensation for this, yet one may choose to take a path unto His Lord.

58. And place your trust in the Ever Living who never dies, and glorify His praises. Sufficient is He as One Ever Aware of the sins of His slaves.

59. The One who created the heavens and the earth, including all that is between them, in six days. Then, He ascended above the throne. The Most Gracious, ask One who is All-Aware about Him[self].

60. And when it is said to them, "Prostrate unto the Most Gracious," they say, "And what is the Most Gracious? Shall we just prostrate unto whatever you command us?" Such only increases them in aversion.

قال تعالى:

﴿وَمَآ أَرْسَلْنَٰكَ إِلَّا مُبَشِّرًا وَنَذِيرًا ۝ قُلْ مَآ أَسْـَٔلُكُمْ عَلَيْهِ مِنْ أَجْرٍ إِلَّا مَن شَآءَ أَن يَتَّخِذَ إِلَىٰ رَبِّهِۦ سَبِيلًا ۝ وَتَوَكَّلْ عَلَى ٱلْحَيِّ ٱلَّذِى لَا يَمُوتُ وَسَبِّحْ بِحَمْدِهِۦ وَكَفَىٰ بِهِۦ بِذُنُوبِ عِبَادِهِۦ خَبِيرًا ۝ ٱلَّذِى خَلَقَ ٱلسَّمَٰوَٰتِ وَٱلْأَرْضَ وَمَا بَيْنَهُمَا فِى سِتَّةِ أَيَّامٍ ثُمَّ ٱسْتَوَىٰ عَلَى ٱلْعَرْشِ ٱلرَّحْمَٰنُ فَسْـَٔلْ بِهِۦ خَبِيرًا ۝ وَإِذَا قِيلَ لَهُمُ ٱسْجُدُواْ لِلرَّحْمَٰنِ قَالُواْ وَمَا ٱلرَّحْمَٰنُ أَنَسْجُدُ لِمَا تَأْمُرُنَا وَزَادَهُمْ نُفُورًا ۝﴾

TAFSEER (EXPLANATION) OF THE VERSES

As your teacher reads the *Tafseer* of al-Imam as-Sa'dee (may Allah have Mercy on him), follow along carefully and take notes on the following points:

1. Not sent to force anyone to accept anything

2. Glad tidings of what?

3. Warnings against what?

4. This necessarily includes:

5. **"Say: I do not ask you for any compensation for this…"**

6. What is the meaning of taking a path unto one's Lord?

7. Such spending in the way of Allah is optional.

8. A command to have ***"tawakkul"***

9. Allah's Name: ***al-Hayy***

10. **"And glorify His praises…"**

11. **"Sufficient is He as One Ever Aware of the sins of His slaves."**

12. The Prophet (صلى الله عليه وسلم) was not sent to watch over them.

13. Allah ascended above the Throne.

14. Allah's Name: *ar-Rahmaan*

15. Verse 59 establishes the following things:

16. **"Ask One who is All-Aware about Him."**

17. People respond one of two ways:

      A.

      B.

18. **"Prostrate unto the Most Gracious..."**

19. The manner of their response

20. The wording of their response

21. Their claim of contradiction in his message

      REVIEW: 17:110

22. Allah has many Names.

23. Every Name includes an Attribute of perfection.

24. **"Shall we just prostrate unto whatever you command us?"**

25. At the core of this question

26. **"<u>Such</u> only increases them..."**

27. They flee from the Truth even more.

TODAY'S VERSES

61. Blessed is He Who placed within the heavens constellations, and He placed therein a lamp and a moon shining with light.

62. And He is the One who has put the night and the day in succession, for anyone who wants to be reminded or wants [to show] gratitude.

قال تعالى:

﴿تَبَارَكَ ٱلَّذِى جَعَلَ فِى ٱلسَّمَآءِ بُرُوجًا وَجَعَلَ فِيهَا سِرَٰجًا وَقَمَرًا مُّنِيرًا ۝ وَهُوَ ٱلَّذِى جَعَلَ ٱلَّيْلَ وَٱلنَّهَارَ خِلْفَةً لِّمَنْ أَرَادَ أَن يَذَّكَّرَ أَوْ أَرَادَ شُكُورًا ۝﴾

TAFSEER (EXPLANATION) OF THE VERSES

As your teacher reads the *Tafseer* of al-Imam as-Sa'dee (may Allah have Mercy on him), follow along carefully and take notes on the following points:

1. This is the third time the word, *"tabaaraka,"* is mentioned in this *soorah*.

    First time:

    Second time:

2. Reviewing the meaning of *"tabaaraka"*

3. A brief overview of the themes of *Soorah al-Furqaan* connected to this word

4. The *"burooj"* of the heavens:

    A.

    B.

5. The *"siraaj"* of the heavens

6. **"And a moon shining with light."**

7. What these things indicate about the Creator

8. The *"khilfah"* of the night and day

9. **"For anyone who wants to be reminded or wants [to show] gratitude."**

10. More specifically: Compensating for missed night prayers

11. The changing conditions of the hearts by day and night

12. Acts of worship performed by day and night

13. Acts of worship are like irrigation.

14. The remaining Verses exemplify His Grace.

TODAY'S VERSE

63. And the real worshippers of the Most Gracious are those who walk the land in humble serenity, and when the foolish address them, they respond with innocent words [keeping them safe from sin].

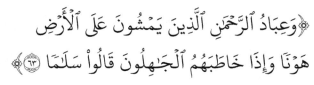

TAFSEER (EXPLANATION) OF THE VERSE

As your teacher reads the *Tafseer* of al-Imam as-Sa'dee (may Allah have Mercy on him), follow along carefully and take notes on the following points:

1. Being an *'abd* (servant) is two categories:

   A.

   19:93

   B.

2. Which one is intended here?

3. Understanding the *"idhaafah"* construction

4. Those who submit and voluntarily worship Allah have the best traits.

5. **"Those who walk the land in humble serenity…"**

6. When the ignorant address them

7. They respond with *"salaam"*

8. This praiseworthy trait includes:

A.

B.

C.

D.

Additional points for consideration and discussion (not from al-Imam as-Sa'dee):

1. This Verse stresses the virtue of restraint, self-control, and graceful interactions.

2. Ramadhaan is the perfect time to develop these important aspects of Islamic character.

3. What other ways does the fast of Ramadhaan help Muslims develop their skills of self-control, discipline, and restraint?

4. Some people might say: "Allah allows us to respond to bad treatment with bad treatment of its like, for example: an insult may be responded to with a similar insult. See Quran 2:194 or 42:40 for example. And the guidance of this Verse in *Soorah al-Furqaan* is only recommended, not obligatory." How would you respond to this?

SINCERE DEVOTION TO OPTIONAL NIGHT PRAYERS

TODAY'S VERSE

64. And those who spend the night focused on their Lord, prostrating and standing [in prayer].

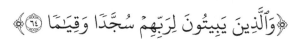

TAFSEER (EXPLANATION) OF THE VERSE*

As your teacher reads the *Tafseer* of al-Imam as-Sa'dee (may Allah have Mercy on him), follow along carefully and take notes on the following points:

1. Spending the night focused on Allah

2. Essential components of that night prayer:

3. A relative passage:

> 32:16

> 32:17

*POINTS 4-11 ARE FROM AL-IMAM AS-SA'DEE'S EXPLANATION OF 32:16-17.

4. **"Their sides forsake their beds..."**

5. **"Calling upon their Lord..."**

6. **"Out of fear and hope..."**

7. They spend from what Allah has provided them with.

8. What kind of spending?

9. The generality of an indefinite noun in a negative context: *"nafs"*

10. **"No soul knows what has been kept hidden for them of joys to the heart..."**

   Hadeeth:

11. **"As a reward for what they used to do."**

SEEKING ALLAH'S PROTECTION FROM THE HELLFIRE

TODAY'S VERSES

65. And those who say: "Our Lord! Keep the punishment of Jahannam from us!" Its punishment is indeed an ongoing penalty.

66. What a terrible abode and place to dwell that is!

قال تعالى:

﴿وَٱلَّذِينَ يَقُولُونَ رَبَّنَا ٱصْرِفْ عَنَّا عَذَابَ جَهَنَّمَ إِنَّ عَذَابَهَا كَانَ غَرَامًا ۝ إِنَّهَا سَآءَتْ مُسْتَقَرًّا وَمُقَامًا ۝﴾

TAFSEER (EXPLANATION) OF THE VERSES*

As your teacher reads the *Tafseer* of al-Imam as-Sa'dee (may Allah have Mercy on him), follow along carefully and take notes on the following points:

1. **"Our Lord! Keep the punishment of Jahannam from us!"**

2. The punishment of Jahannam is **"gharaam"**.

3. Why do they say, **"What a terrible abode and place to dwell that is"**?

    A.

    B.

    C.

On the authority of Anas ibn Maalik: The Messenger of Allah -may Allah raise his rank and grant him peace- said: "**Whoever asks Allah for Paradise three times, Paradise says: 'O Allah, grant him entrance to Paradise!' And whoever seeks refuge with Allah from the Hellfire three times, the Hellfire says: 'O Allah, grant him refuge from the Hellfire!'**" [It was collected by Ahmad, at-Tirmithee, and Ibn Maajah; al-Albaanee authenticated it.]

عَنْ أَنَسِ بْنِ مَالِكٍ قَالَ: قَالَ رَسُولُ اللهِ صَلَّى اللهُ عَلَيْهِ وَسَلَّمَ: «مَنْ سَأَلَ اللهَ الْجَنَّةَ ثَلَاثًا، قَالَتِ الْجَنَّةُ: اللَّهُمَّ أَدْخِلْهُ الْجَنَّةَ؛ وَمَنِ اسْتَعَاذَ بِاللهِ مِنَ النَّارِ ثَلَاثًا، قَالَتِ النَّارُ: اللَّهُمَّ أَعِذْهُ مِنَ النَّارِ!» أَخْرَجَهُ أَحْمَدُ، وَالتِّرْمِذِيُّ، وَابْنُ مَاجَهْ، وَصَحَّحَهُ الْأَلْبَانِيُّ.

Points to consider from this hadeeth:

1. The importance of asking Allah for Paradise.

2. Paradise has already been created; it hears and speaks.

3. The importance of seeking Allah's protection from Hell.

4. The Hellfire has already been created; it hears and speaks.

5. Other attributes of the Hellfire:

> 25:12

> 67:8

> Hadeeth:

6. Ramadhaan is a great season of being saved from the Hellfire.

> Hadeeth:

7. A reminder about a neglected Sunnah mentioned in Lesson 6 (Point 12)

> Hadeeth:

MODERATION & BALANCE IN ONE'S FINANCIAL AFFAIRS

TODAY'S VERSE

67. And when they spend, they are neither extravagant nor miserly, but they take a middle course between those [extremes].

قال تعالى:

﴿وَٱلَّذِينَ إِذَآ أَنفَقُواْ لَمْ يُسْرِفُواْ وَلَمْ يَقْتُرُواْ وَكَانَ بَيْنَ ذَٰلِكَ قَوَامًا ٦٧﴾

TAFSEER (EXPLANATION) OF THE VERSE*

As your teacher reads the *Tafseer* of al-Imam as-Sa'dee (may Allah have Mercy on him), follow along carefully and take notes on the following points:

1. Which kinds of spending?

2. The consequences of spending too much

3. The consequences of not spending enough

4. **"They take a middle course between those [extremes]."**

On the authority of Ibn 'Abbaas (may Allah be pleased with him): The Messenger of Allah (may Allah raise his rank and grant him peace) was the most generous of all people in [sharing] good things. He would get even more generous in the month of Ramadhaan. Jibreel (may Allah grant him peace) would meet him every year in Ramadhaan until it would end; the Messenger of Allah (may Allah raise his rank and grant him peace) would recite Quran to him. When he would meet up with Jibreel, the Messenger of Allah (may Allah raise his rank and grant him peace) would be more generous than the flowing wind. [Agreed upon]

عَنِ ابْنِ عَبَّاسٍ ــ رَضِيَ اللهُ عَنْهُمَا ــ ، قَالَ: كَانَ رَسُولُ اللهِ ــ صَلَّى اللهُ عَلَيْهِ وَسَلَّمَ ــ أَجْوَدَ النَّاسِ بِالخَيْرِ، وَكَانَ أَجْوَدَ مَا يَكُونُ فِي شَهْرِ رَمَضَانَ. إِنَّ جِبْرِيلَ ــ عَلَيْهِ السَّلَامُ ــ كَانَ يَلْقَاهُ فِي كُلِّ سَنَةٍ فِي رَمَضَانَ حَتَّى يَنْسَلِخَ، فَيَعْرِضُ عَلَيْهِ رَسُولُ اللهِ ــ صَلَّى اللهُ عَلَيْهِ وَسَلَّمَ ــ الْقُرْآنَ، فَإِذَا لَقِيَهُ جِبْرِيلُ كَانَ رَسُولُ اللهِ ــ صَلَّى اللهُ عَلَيْهِ وَسَلَّمَ ــ أَجْوَدَ بِالخَيْرِ مِنَ الرِّيحِ الْمُرْسَلَةِ. مُتَّفَقٌ عَلَيْهِ.

Points to consider from this hadeeth:

1. An encouragement to be generous in the month of Ramadhaan.

2. The Quran is supposed to have an important impact on a Muslim's behavior.

3. The Quran should be reviewed with a teacher, especially in Ramadhaan.

4. Virtuous actions are appropriate for virtuous times.

5. The more pious a person is, the more he focuses on the Hereafter and the less he focuses on (unnecessary) worldly matters.

AVOIDING POLYTHEISM & DESTRUCTIVE MAJOR SINS

TODAY'S VERSES

قال تعالى:

68. And those who do not call upon any other deity along with Allah, nor do they take any life which Allah has forbidden, except with just cause, nor do they fornicate. Whoever does that shall encounter punishment for sin!

69. The punishment will be multiplied on him on the Day of Resurrection; he will abide therein in disgrace.

﴿وَٱلَّذِينَ لَا يَدۡعُونَ مَعَ ٱللَّهِ إِلَٰهًا ءَاخَرَ وَلَا يَقۡتُلُونَ ٱلنَّفۡسَ ٱلَّتِي حَرَّمَ ٱللَّهُ إِلَّا بِٱلۡحَقِّ وَلَا يَزۡنُونَۚ وَمَن يَفۡعَلۡ ذَٰلِكَ يَلۡقَ أَثَامًا ۝ يُضَٰعَفۡ لَهُ ٱلۡعَذَابُ يَوۡمَ ٱلۡقِيَٰمَةِ وَيَخۡلُدۡ فِيهِۦ مُهَانًا ۝﴾

TAFSEER (EXPLANATION) OF THE VERSES

As your teacher reads the *Tafseer* of al-Imam as-Sa'dee (may Allah have Mercy on him), follow along carefully and take notes on the following points:

1. The true servants of ar-Rahmaan do not supplicate to other than Allah.

2. What is "**any life which Allah has forbidden**"?

3. What are some examples of a "**just cause**"?

4. "**Nor do they fornicate...**"

   23:6

   70:30

5. "**Whoever does THAT...**"

6. The punishment of *"Athaam"* is explained:

7. The threat of eternal or ongoing punishment

8. The threat applies to all three crimes mentioned.

9. The *"khulood"* (eternalness) of the punishment is restricted.

10. These three are the most serious major sins.

11. The corruption caused by these three crimes:

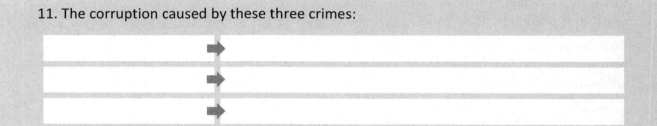

THE GREAT STATUS OF TOWBAH (GENUINE REPENTANCE)

TODAY'S VERSES

قال تعالى:

70. But not those who repent, believe, and do righteous deeds, for such people, Allah replaces their sins with good deeds, and Allah is Oft-Forgiving, Ever Merciful.

71. And whoever repents and does righteous deeds, then he truly repents unto Allah with genuine repentance.

﴿إِلَّا مَن تَابَ وَءَامَنَ وَعَمِلَ عَمَلًا صَلِحًا فَأُوْلَٰٓئِكَ يُبَدِّلُ ٱللَّهُ سَيِّـَٔاتِهِمْ حَسَنَٰتٍ وَكَانَ ٱللَّهُ غَفُورًا رَّحِيمًا ۝ وَمَن تَابَ وَعَمِلَ صَلِحًا فَإِنَّهُۥ يَتُوبُ إِلَى ٱللَّهِ مَتَابًا ۝﴾

TAFSEER (EXPLANATION) OF THE VERSES

As your teacher reads the *Tafseer* of al-Imam as-Sa'dee (may Allah have Mercy on him), follow along carefully and take notes on the following points:

1. **"But not those who repent…"**

2. The three main steps of true repentance:

3. Repentance paired with *eemaan* (faith)

4. Repentance and *eemaan* paired with righteous actions

5. The replacement of sins with good deeds

6. The story of the man who asks about some of his sins that are missing from his record

    Hadeeth:

7. From Allah's Names: *al-Ghafoor*

8. From Allah's Names: *ar-Raheem*

9. **"Then he truly repents unto Allah with genuine repentance."**

10. Essential advice

11. The overall goal of these two Verses

TODAY'S VERSE

قال تعالى:

72. And [they are] those who do not witness falsehood, and if they [even] pass by some frivolity, they pass by with dignity.

﴿وَٱلَّذِينَ لَا يَشْهَدُونَ ٱلزُّورَ وَإِذَا مَرُّواْ بِٱللَّغْوِ مَرُّواْ كِرَامًا ۝٧٢﴾

TAFSEER (EXPLANATION) OF THE VERSE*

As your teacher reads the *Tafseer* of al-Imam as-Sa'dee (may Allah have Mercy on him), follow along carefully and take notes on the following points:

1. Not even "witnessing" falsehood

2. What is the meaning of *"zoor"*?

3. The overall meaning:

4. Examples of the kinds of gatherings they actively avoid:

1.	7.
2.	8.
3.	9.
4.	10.
5.	11.
6.	

5. A meaning of the Verse, understood by way of *"fah-wal-khitaab"*

6. *"Shahaadat az-Zoor"* vs. *"Qowl az-Zoor"*

*Reminder: Qowl az-Zoor in Ramadhaan?!

7. **"If they pass by some <u>frivolity</u>..."**

8. **"They pass by with dignity."**

    A. What they do:

    B. What they believe about that frivolity:

9. The language indicates the incidental nature of this interaction.

10. A very important quote from a number of early imams of *Tafseer*

    A. Who were they?

    B. What did they say?

    C. What days would this apply to in our local culture? (three examples)

        1.

        2.

        3.

11. The basis for saying that a specific issue is "in the Quran", meaning: under a generality

    Hadeeth:

TODAY'S VERSE

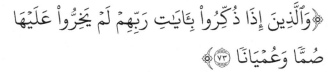

قال تعالى:

73. And [they are] those who, when reminded of the aayaat (signs and Verses) of their Lord, they do not turn away from that, [pretending to be] deaf and blind.

﴿وَٱلَّذِينَ إِذَا ذُكِّرُواْ بِـَٔايَٰتِ رَبِّهِمْ لَمْ يَخِرُّواْ عَلَيْهَا صُمًّا وَعُمْيَانًا ٧٣﴾

TAFSEER (EXPLANATION) OF THE VERSE*

As your teacher reads the *Tafseer* of al-Imam as-Sa'dee (may Allah have Mercy on him), follow along carefully and take notes on the following points:

1. "Those who, when reminded of the aayaat of their Lord…"

2. What they do not do in this situation

3. What they actually do in that situation

      32:15

      Submission and compliance

4. Four amazing effects:

*POINTS 5-7 ARE NOT FROM AL-IMAM AS-SA'DEE'S EXPLANATION OF 25:73.

5. Another description of how believers respond to the Quran being recited

      8:2

6. The importance of being quiet and paying attention to the Quran

    7:204

    What was this verse revealed about?

    How broadly does it apply?

7. Using the Verse (32: 15) to establish prostrating every time the Quran is heard

    The generality of the wording

    Vs. the application of the Companions

    The point: Is everyone who has an *aayah* within his argument to be respected?

    3:7

    Hadeeth:

TODAY'S VERSE

74. And [they are] those who say, "Our Lord, give us among our mates and offspring what will be a comfort to our eyes, and make us leading examples for the pious."

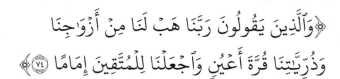

TAFSEER (EXPLANATION) OF THE VERSE

As your teacher reads the *Tafseer* of al-Imam as-Sa'dee (may Allah have Mercy on him), follow along carefully and take notes on the following points:

1. The meaning of the word, *"azwaaj"*

2. The meaning of the phrase, *"qurrat a'yun"*

3. What this means in reality: how they would actually be

4. What this also necessarily includes

   Based on the phrase:

5. How this transcends broadly into the whole society

*What **must** be behind all of that? *[additional benefit, not from al-Imam as-Sa'dee]*

6. **"Make us leading examples for the pious..."**

*Does this Verse justify seeking positions of authority? [not from al-Imam as-Sa'dee]

Reminder: Is every opinion accompanied by a Verse respected?

Hadeeth:

Hadeeth:

7. More details about what is included in this supplication

32:24

Deeds

Patience

Knowledge

The resulting rank:

8. Thus, they deserve what is mentioned in the next Verse.

LOFTY ABODES, PURE GREETINGS, & ETERNAL SAFETY

TODAY'S VERSES

75. Such are rewarded with lofty abodes [in Paradise], a result of their patience. They are met therein with greetings and safety.

76. Abiding therein forever; what a fine abode and place to dwell!

قال تعالى:

﴿أُوْلَـٰٓئِكَ يُجْزَوْنَ ٱلْغُرْفَةَ بِمَا صَبَرُواْ وَيُلَقَّوْنَ فِيهَا تَحِيَّةً وَسَلَـٰمًا ۝ خَـٰلِدِينَ فِيهَا حَسُنَتْ مُسْتَقَرًّا وَمُقَامًا ۝﴾

TAFSEER (EXPLANATION) OF THE VERSES

As your teacher reads the *Tafseer* of al-Imam as-Sa'dee (may Allah have Mercy on him), follow along carefully and take notes on the following points:

1. **"Such are rewarded with lofty abodes..."**

2. The great reward of patience

       13:23

       13:24

3. Greetings from whom?

4. Greetings along with *"salaam"*

5. **REVIEW:** A summary of these great attributes from Verses 63-74

1.	5.	9.
2.	6.	10.
3.	7.	11.
4.	8.	12.

13.	22.	30.
14.	23.	31.
15.	24.	32.
16.	25.	33.
17.	26.	34.
18.	27.	35.
19.	28.	36.
20.	29.	37.
21.		

6. **REFLECTION:** How amazing that is!

7. The great Favor of Allah in granting these kinds of ranks

8. The great blessing of being guided to the steps needed

9. Another beautiful supplication from al-Imam as-Sa'dee (may Allah have Mercy on him):

فَاللَّهُمَّ لَكَ الْحَمْدُ، وَإِلَيْكَ الْمُشْتَكَى، وَأَنْتَ الْمُسْتَعَانُ، وَبِكَ الْمُسْتَغَاثُ، وَلَا حَوْلَ وَلَا قُوَّةَ إِلَّا بِكَ، لَا نَمْلِكُ لِأَنْفُسِنَا نَفْعًا وَلَا ضَرًّا، وَلَا نَقْدِرُ عَلَى مِثْقَالِ ذَرَّةٍ مِنَ الْخَيْرِ إِنَ لَمْ تُيَسِّرْ ذَلِكَ لَنَا، فَإِنَّا ضُعَفَاءُ عَاجِزُونَ مِنْ كُلِّ وَجْهٍ. نَشْهَدُ أَنَّكَ إِنْ وَكَلْتَنَا إِلَى أَنْفُسِنَا طَرْفَةَ عَيْنٍ وَكَلْتَنَا إِلَى ضَعْفٍ وَعَجْزٍ وَخَطِيئَةٍ، فَلَا نَثِقُ يَا رَبَّنَا إِلَّا بِرَحْمَتِكَ الَّتِي بِهَا خَلَقْتَنَا وَرَزَقْتَنَا وَأَنْعَمْتَ عَلَيْنَا بِمَا أَنْعَمْتَ مِنَ النِّعَمِ الظَّاهِرَةِ وَالْبَاطِنَةِ وَصَرَفْتَ عَنَّا مِنَ النِّقَمِ، فَارْحَمْنَا رَحْمَةً تُغْنِينَا بِهَا عَنْ رَحْمَةِ مَنْ سِوَاكَ، فَلَا خَابَ مَنْ سَأَلَكَ وَرَجَاكَ.

NEVER-ENDING PUNISHMENT FOR REJECTING THE TRUTH

TODAY'S VERSE

77. Say: My Lord would have paid you no attention, had it not been for your supplications [to Him]. Yet you have indeed rejected [the truth], and so it shall be never-ending punishment.

قال تعالى:

﴿قُلْ مَا يَعْبَؤُاْ بِكُمْ رَبِّي لَوْلَا دُعَآؤُكُمْ ۖ فَقَدْ كَذَّبْتُمْ فَسَوْفَ يَكُونُ لِزَامًا ٧٧﴾

TAFSEER (EXPLANATION) OF THE VERSE

As your teacher reads the *Tafseer* of al-Imam as-Sa'dee (may Allah have Mercy on him), follow along carefully and take notes on the following points:

1. Dispelling a false notion that might arise

2. No attention or concern

3. Their supplications [of *towheed*] were actually meaningful.

4. Otherwise no concern or love

5. The meaning of *"Lizaam"*

6. The Judgment of Allah is coming. *[Remember the name of the Soorah!]*

7. Concluding the explanation of *Soorah al-Furqaan*

AL-HAMDU LILLAAH

All praise is due to Allah! This completes our study of these 77 beautiful verses of this amazing chapter, *Soorah al-Furqaan*. May Allah accept these efforts of ours, as well as our fasting and praying, and may He forgive our sins and allow us entrance to His Paradise. Indeed, His Promise is true!

إِنَّ ٱلَّذِينَ ءَامَنُوا۟ وَعَمِلُوا۟ ٱلصَّٰلِحَٰتِ يَهْدِيهِمْ رَبُّهُم بِإِيمَٰنِهِمْ تَجْرِى مِن تَحْتِهِمُ ٱلْأَنْهَٰرُ فِى جَنَّٰتِ ٱلنَّعِيمِ ۹ دَعْوَىٰهُمْ فِيهَا سُبْحَٰنَكَ ٱللَّهُمَّ وَتَحِيَّتُهُمْ فِيهَا سَلَٰمٌ وَءَاخِرُ دَعْوَىٰهُمْ أَنِ ٱلْحَمْدُ لِلَّهِ رَبِّ ٱلْعَٰلَمِينَ ۱۰

سورة يونس

Verily those who have believed and worked righteous deeds, their Lord guides them by their faith. Rivers flow from under them in gardens of joy. Their call therein is: *"Subhaanak Allaahumma"* (Exalted You are, O Allah). And their greeting therein is *salaam* (peace). And the last of their call is: "All praise is due to Allah, Lord of all things." [10:9-10]

ٱلْحَمْدُ لِلَّه
رَبِّ ٱلْعَٰلَمِينَ

QUIZ 1: REVIEW QUESTIONS

The following questions are designed to test your understanding of the first 20 Verses of Soorah al-Furqaan and the explanation of al-Imam as-Sa'dee. After taking the quiz on your own, check your answers with the Answer Key on p.93.

1. How does al-Imam as-Sa'dee classify *Soorah al-Furqaan*?

    A. *Makkiyyah* by consensus

    B. *Madaniyyah* by consensus

    C. *Makkiyyah* according to the majority of scholars

    D. *Madaniyyah* according to the majority of scholars

2. What is the meaning of *"al-Furqaan"* according to al-Imam as-Sa'dee?

    A. the criterion between halaal and haraam

    B. the criterion between guidance and misguidance

    C. the criterion between the people of Paradise and the people of Hell

    D. all of the above

3. In *Soorah al-Furqaan*, how does Allah disqualify false deities from being things rightfully worshipped?

    A. that they have lied upon the prophets of Allah

    B. that they are incapable of harm or benefit

    C. that they eat, drink, and walk about in the marketplaces

    D. all of the above

4. In Verses 5 and 6, Allah mentions the claim of the pagans, that the Prophet (may Allah raise his rank and grant him peace) was writing down the Quran as dictated to him from someone morning and night, and then Allah says that He is Forgiving and Merciful. What does al-Imam as-Sa'dee deduce about the connection between these ideas?

    A. Allah encourages them to take a path towards forgiveness and mercy.

    B. They will never attain Allah's Forgiveness or Mercy.

    C. They are already forgiven for their false claims.

    D. All of the creation receives Allah's Forgiveness and Mercy in the Hereafter.

5. Why did the polytheists say, **"What is with this messenger, eating food and walking in the marketplaces?"**

    A. It was just one of their many lies they invented to discredit him.

    B. They were trying to prove he was not worthy of worship.

    C. They were praising him for his good manners when mixing with the people.

    D. They were trying to prove he could not actually be a prophet.

6. In his explanation of Verse 12 which means, **"They hear its furious rage and roar,"** how does al-Imam as-Sa'dee explain the anger of the Hellfire?

    A. It is not real anger; it is only a loud crackling sound.
    B. It is angry with the disbelievers because its Creator is angry with them.
    C. When a fire "rages", that means it burns intensely, so it is only allegorical.
    D. It yells at the disbelievers and rebukes them for their disbelief.

7. Which of the following objections were raised by the polytheists about the Quran, as mentioned in *Soorah al-Furqaan*?

    A. It should have been revealed all at once, in a single revelation.
    B. It should have been revealed in Greek, the language of enlightenment.
    C. It should have been revealed to one of the two great men of the villages.
    D. all of the above

8. Regarding Verse 15, which means: **"Say: Is THAT better or the Garden of Eternity promised to the pious?"** How does al-Imam as-Sa'dee explain this Verse?

    A. **"THAT"** is a reference to their lies and slander.
    B. **"THAT"** is ambiguous and refers to whatever the reader imagines.
    C. **"THAT"** refers to the beautiful gardens and treasures of this worldly life.
    D. none of the above

9. In Verse 17, whom does Allah address, saying [what means]: **"Was it you who misled these servants of Mine?"**

    A. the disbelievers specifically
    B. the angels and jinn specifically
    C. all things worshipped without right, in general
    D. the jinn and humankind in general

10. How does the meaning of Verse 20, **"And We sent no messengers before you except that they actually ate food and walked in marketplaces..."** connect to one of the previous Verses in the *Soorah*?

    A. It explains the rage of the Hellfire mentioned in Verse 12.
    B. It clarifies one of the ways the polytheists tried to discredit the Prophet. ﷺ
    C. It clarifies one of the lies against the Prophet, that he did not eat food.
    D. It proves that all previous messengers had been either jinn or angels.

ANSWER KEY: See p.93.

QUIZ 2: REVIEW QUESTIONS

The following questions are designed to test your understanding of Verses 21-43 of Soorah al-Furqaan and the explanation of al-Imam as-Sa'dee. After taking the quiz on your own, check your answers with the Answer Key on p.93.

1. An example of the disbelievers being given what they asked for, as found in *Soorah al-Furqaan*, would be:

      A. that Allah revealed the Quran all at once

      B. that Allah sent the angel Jibreel to warn the people along with Muhammad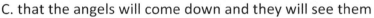

      C. that the angels will come down and they will see them

      D. none of the above

2. How does al-Imam as-Sa'dee explain the rest and relaxation in Paradise being described as **"better than"** the situation of the people in Hell, as found in Verse 24?

      A. The rest and relaxation in Hell is minimal and not very fulfilling.

      B. People in Hell will sleep on beds of fire in ovens.

      C. Something can be "better than" something devoid of any good.

      D. "Better than" actually means "**not** better than"

3. How does al-Imam as-Sa'dee explain the arrival of the angels, as mentioned in Verse 25?

      A. They descend and form one single row, surrounding everyone.

      B. They descend from each of the heavens, forming multiple rows.

      C. neither A nor B

      D. maybe A or B

4. What deduction does al-Imam as-Sa'dee make from Verse 26 [which means], **"For the disbelievers it is a day of difficulty."**

      A. Murderers will find no safety on that day.

      B. All kings and leaders will be humiliated and destroyed.

      C. It is also a day of difficulty for the believers.

      D. none of the above

5. What reason does Allah provide for the Quran being revealed in stages?

      A. All previous books of revelation were sent down in stages as well.

      B. This would make the Prophet's heart firm.

      C. How else would we have "Makkiyyah" and "Madaniyyah" Verses?

      D. all of the above

6. What advice does al-Imam as-Sa'dee offer teachers, based on how Allah revealed the Quran in stages?

    A. They should defend the honor of their students when they are slandered.
    B. They should expect a high level of respect from their students.
    C. They should address students with things relevant to their immediate situation.
    D. all of the above

7. Which passage best highlights the importance of righteous companionship?

    A. Verses 27-29 about the oppressor biting at his hand
    B. Verse 24 about the superiority of the rest and relaxation in Paradise
    C. Verse 25 about the sky splitting open
    D. Verse 32 about the Quran being sent down in stages

8. How does al-Imam as-Sa'dee explain Verse 34 [which means], **"Those gathered upon their faces unto Jahannam…"**

    A. They are pulled and dragged, in disgrace, by angels of punishment.
    B. Their faces will be ripped apart, dragged over sharp rocks.
    C. Their faces will be the size of entire planets.
    D. all of the above

9. What was the purpose of the polytheists asking, **"Is this the one whom Allah has sent as a Messenger?"** as found in Verse 41?

    A. They were trying to find out the identity of the Messenger.
    B. They were mocking the angel, Jibreel.
    C. They were mocking the Messenger of Allah.
    D. They did not believe in the existence of Allah.

10. Complete the meaning of Verse 43 from *Soorah al-Furqaan*: **"Have you seen him who has taken _____ as his god? Could you then be responsible for him?"**

    A. the moon
    B. his own whims
    C. his religious leaders
    D. rocks and trees

ANSWER KEY: See p.93.

QUIZ 3: REVIEW QUESTIONS

The following questions are designed to test your understanding of Verses 44-64 of Soorah al-Furqaan and the explanation of al-Imam as-Sa'dee. After taking the quiz on your own, check your answers with the Answer Key on p.93.

1. Complete the meaning of Verse 44 from *Soorah al-Furqaan*: **"Or do you assume that most of them [actually] listen or comprehend? They are only like _____, or yet even further astray!"**

      A. donkeys
      B. monkeys
      C. cattle
      D. devils

2. Which of the following benefits does al-Imam as-Sa'dee extract from the movement of the sun and the shadows, as mentioned in Verse 46?

      A. This shows us something about the Power and Capability of Allah.
      B. This proves that Allah alone deserves worship.
      C. This shows us something about the Mercy and Greatness of Allah.
      D. all of the above

3. In Verse 47, Allah says that He made the night to be *"subaat."* What does that mean?

      A. something which provides stability
      B. a time for relaxation and sleep
      C. Saturday is an official day of rest, called: *Yowm as-Sabt.*
      D. a time for increased energy and serious activity

4. What is mentioned as a good sign before the arrival of Allah's Mercy in Verse 48? How does al-Imam as-Sa'dee explain the specific meaning of Allah's Mercy in this Verse?

      A. Winds are good tidings of the coming rain, which is from Allah's Mercy.
      B. Rain is good tidings of the coming crops, which are from Allah's Mercy.
      C. Both winds and rain take place before the Day of Judgement, a day of Mercy.
      D. All tragedies in general are good tidings of imminent Mercy for the believers.

5. As explained in class, what is very special about the mention of *"jihaad"* in Verse 52?

      A. Military opposition was actually allowed in the later Makkan period.
      B. It proves that military opposition is the only correct meaning of *jihaad.*
      C. It proves that *jihaad* is an obligation, whether prepared or not.
      D. It proves that *jihaad* is not limited to military opposition; it includes *da'wah.*

6. In Verse 53, Allah mentions the two kinds of water on earth and the hidden barrier between them. What other *Soorah* also mentions this?

    A. *Soorah an-Noor*
    B. *Soorah ar-Rahmaan*
    C. *Soorah al-Burooj*
    D. *Soorah al-Mulk*

7. Complete the meaning of Verse 54: **"And He is the One who created humankind from water, and He has made relatives for him through blood lineage and _____..."**

    A. trade
    B. traveling
    C. marriage
    D. breastfeeding

8. In Verse 59, Allah commands His Prophet (may Allah raise his rank and grant him peace) to ask someone about Him, someone who is **"khabeer"** (well-informed). Who is intended by this description, as explained by al-Imam as-Sa'dee?

    A. Allah Himself
    B. Jibreel, the Angel of Revelation
    C. Aboo Bakr as-Siddeeq
    D. 'Abdullah ibn Salaam

9. What is correct about Verse 61, which means: **"Blessed is He Who placed within the heavens constellations, and He placed therein a lamp and a moon shining with light."**

    A. It includes the third time the word, **"tabaaraka,"** is used in this *soorah*.
    B. This proves that the word, *Furqaan*, refers to the sun, moon, and stars.
    C. The lamp is the moon itself; the "moon shining with light" is actually the sun.
    D. all of the above

10. How does al-Imam as-Sa'dee explain the word, **"salaam,"** in Verse 63, which means: **"When the foolish address them, they respond with 'salaam'..."**

    A. Believers say, *"as-Salaamu 'alaykum,"* as they depart the company of fools.
    B. Believers respond to fools with graceful and innocent words, avoiding sin.
    C. Believers respond to foolishness with similar foolishness.
    D. It proves the obligation to respond to the greetings of non-Muslims.

ANSWER KEY: See p.93.

QUIZ 4: REVIEW QUESTIONS

The following questions are designed to test your understanding of Verses 66-74 of Soorah al-Furqaan and the explanation of al-Imam as-Sa'dee. After taking the quiz on your own, check your answers with the Answer Key on p.93.

1. In Verse 65, the believers supplicate: **"Our Lord! Keep the punishment of Jahannam from us!"** How did al-Imam as-Sa'dee explain this supplication?

    A. It means: Keep us away from the paths that lead to it (in the future).
    B. It means: Forgive us of our behavior which warrants it (from the past).
    C. both A and B
    D. neither A nor B

2. Allah praises the believers who spend their money, without extravagance or miserliness. This includes:

    A. obligatory spending, like taking care of the financial needs of one's family
    B. the payment of zakaat
    C. charity which is recommended but not required
    D. all of the above

3. Which of the sins mentioned in Verse 68 causes a person to go to Hell eternally?

    A. calling upon other than Allah (with *du'aa'*)
    B. murder
    C. fornication and adultery
    D. all of the above

4. Complete the statement of al-Imam as-Sa'dee: *"Shirk corrupts the religion, murder ruins physical safety, and fornication destroys _____."*

    A. physical health and well-being
    B. people's honor
    C. family ties
    D. communities

5. How does al-Imam as-Sa'dee explain the exchange of evil deeds for good ones mentioned in Verse 70?

    A. Their sinful behavior of the past is turned into good deeds after repentance.
    B. Their sinful behavior planned for the future is fulfilled but forgiven anyway.
    C. both A and B
    D. neither A nor B

6. What is the case of the man who says on the Day of Judgment, *"My Lord! I have some sins that I do not see here!"*?

        A. This is about major sins which he repented from.
        B. This is about sins which were mistakenly put on someone else's account.
        C. This is about a man who wants to be punished for his sins.
        D. This is said by a man who remains in Hell forever.

7. Regarding Verse 72 [which means]: **"And those who do not witness *zoor*…"** How does al-Imam as-Sa'dee explain *"zoor"*?

        A. impermissible statements and actions (in general)
        B. any speech devoid of benefit
        C. the holidays of the disbelievers
        D. all of the above

8. Complete the meaning of Verse 73: **"And [they are] those who, when reminded of the *aayaat* (signs and Verses) of their Lord, _____."**

        A. they fall to the ground in prostration, crying
        B. their hearts tremble in fear and they are increased in faith
        C. they do not turn away, deaf and blind
        D. they close their eyes in deep contemplation

9. What was an important deduction made by al-Imam as-Sa'dee about the believers and how they supplicate for their wives and offspring to be a pleasure to their eyes?

        A. This includes that they would be obedient and knowledgeable.
        B. This means he must purchase beauty supplies for them.
        C. This Verse justifies seeking positions of leadership in some cases.
        D. both A and C

10. Which of the following is **NOT** one of the praiseworthy traits of the true worshippers of Allah indicated in Verses 63-74?

        A. They respond to bad treatment with grace and restraint.
        B. They fast the month of Ramadhaan.
        C. They pay their *zakaat* in full.
        D. They stand at night in optional prayers.

ANSWER KEY: See p.93.

QUIZ: COMPREHENSIVE REVIEW QUESTIONS

The following questions are designed to test your understanding of Soorah al-Furqaan and the explanation of al-Imam as-Sa'dee. After taking the quiz on your own, check your answers with the Answer Key on p.93.

1. How does al-Imam as-Sa'dee classify *Soorah al-Furqaan*?

    A. *Makkiyyah* by consensus
    B. *Madaniyyah* according to the majority of scholars
    C. *Makkiyyah* according to the majority of scholars
    D. *Madaniyyah* by consensus

2. What is the meaning of *"al-Furqaan"* according to al-Imam as-Sa'dee?

    A. the criterion between halaal and haraam
    B. the criterion between guidance and misguidance
    C. the criterion between the people of Paradise and the people of Hell
    D. all of the above

3. In Verses 5 and 6, Allah mentions the claim of the pagans, that the Prophet (may Allah raise his rank and grant him peace) was writing down the Quran as dictated to him from someone morning and night, and then Allah says that He is Forgiving and Merciful. What does al-Imam as-Sa'dee deduce about the connection between these ideas?

    A. Allah encourages them to take a path towards forgiveness and mercy.
    B. They will never attain Allah's Forgiveness or Mercy.
    C. They are already forgiven for their false claims.
    D. All of the creation receives Allah's Forgiveness and Mercy in the Hereafter.

4. In his explanation of Verse 12 which means, **"They hear its furious rage and roar,"** how does al-Imam as-Sa'dee explain the anger of the Hellfire?

    A. It is not real anger; it is only a loud crackling sound.
    B. It is angry with the disbelievers because its Creator is angry with them.
    C. When a fire "rages", that means it burns intensely, so it is only allegorical.
    D. It yells at the disbelievers and rebukes them for their disbelief.

5. Which of the following objections were raised by the polytheists about the Quran, as mentioned in *Soorah al-Furqaan*?

    A. It should have been revealed in stages, instead of one single revelation.
    B. It should have been revealed in Hebrew, the language of previous prophets.
    C. It should have been revealed to one of the two great men of the villages.
    D. none of the above

6. In Verse 17, whom does Allah address, saying [what means]: **"Was it you who misled these servants of Mine?"**

    A. the disbelievers specifically
    B. the angels and jinn specifically
    C. all false objects of worship in general
    D. the jinn and humankind in general

7. How does al-Imam as-Sa'dee explain the arrival of the angels, as mentioned in Verse 25?

    A. They descend and form one single row, surrounding everyone.
    B. They descend from each of the heavens, forming only three rows.
    C. neither A nor B
    D. both A and B

8. What deduction does al-Imam as-Sa'dee make from Verse 26 [which means], **"For the disbelievers it is a day of difficulty."**

    A. Murderers will find no safety on that day.
    B. All kings and leaders will be humiliated and destroyed.
    C. It is an easy day for the believers.
    D. none of the above

9. What advice does al-Imam as-Sa'dee offer teachers, based on how Allah revealed the Quran in stages?

    A. They should defend the honor of their students when they are slandered.
    B. They should expect a high level of respect from their students.
    C. They should address students with things relevant to their immediate situation.
    D. all of the above

10. Which passage best highlights the importance of shunning evil companionship?

    A. Verse 25 about the sky splitting open
    B. Verse 24 about the superiority of the rest and relaxation in Paradise
    C. Verses 27-29 about the oppressors biting at their hands
    D. Verse 32 about the Quran being sent down in stages

11. How does al-Imam as-Sa'dee explain Verse 34 [which means], **"Those gathered upon their faces unto Jahannam…"**

    A. They are pulled and dragged, in disgrace, by angels of punishment.
    B. Their faces will be scraped with iron hooks.
    C. Their faces will be the size of mountains.
    D. all of the above

12. Complete the meaning of Verse 43 from *Soorah al-Furqaan*: **"Have you seen him who has taken _____ as his god? Could you then be responsible for him?"**

    A. the sun
    B. his wife
    C. his own whims
    D. his prophet

13. Which of the following benefits does al-Imam as-Sa'dee extract from the movement of the sun and the shadows, as mentioned in Verse 46?

A. This shows us something about the Power and Capability of Allah.
B. This proves that Allah alone deserves worship.
C. This shows us something about the Mercy and Greatness of Allah.
D. all of the above

14. In Verse 47, Allah says that He made the night to be *"subaat."* What does that mean?

A. something which provides stability
B. a time for relaxation and sleep
C. Saturday is an official day of rest, called: *Yowm as-Sabt.*
D. a time for increased energy and serious activity

15. As explained in class, what is very special about the mention of *"jihaad"* in Verse 52?

A. Military opposition was actually allowed in the later Makkan period.
B. It proves that military opposition is the only correct meaning of *jihaad.*
C. It proves that *jihaad* is an obligation, whether prepared or not.
D. It proves that *jihaad* is not limited to military opposition; it includes *da'wah.*

16. In Verse 59, Allah commands His Prophet (may Allah raise his rank and grant him peace) to ask someone about Him, someone who is *"khabeer"* (well-informed). Who is intended by this description, as explained by al-Imam as-Sa'dee?

A. Allah Himself
B. Moosaa ibn 'Emraan
C. 'Alee ibn Abee Taalib
D. any Jew in al-Madeenah

17. What is correct about Verse 61, which means: **"Blessed is He Who placed within the heavens constellations, and He placed therein a lamp and a moon shining with light."**

A. It includes the third time the word, *"tabaaraka,"* is used in this *soorah.*
B. This proves that the word, *Furqaan,* refers to the sun, moon, and stars.
C. The lamp is the moon itself; the "moon shining with light" is actually the sun.
D. all of the above

18. How does al-Imam as-Sa'dee explain the word, *"salaam,"* in Verse 63, which means: **"When the foolish address them, they respond with 'salaam'…"**

A. Believers say, *"as-Salaamu 'alaykum,"* as they depart the company of fools.
B. Believers respond to fools with graceful and innocent words, avoiding sin.
C. Believers respond to foolishness with similar foolishness.
D. It proves the obligation to respond to the greetings of non-Muslims.

19. In Verse 65, the believers supplicate: *"Our Lord! Keep the punishment of Jahannam from us!"* How did al-Imam as-Sa'dee explain this supplication?

A. It means: Keep us away from the paths that lead to it (in the future).
B. It means: Forgive us of our behavior which warrants it (from the past).
C. neither A nor B
D. both A and B

20. Which of the sins mentioned in Verse 68 causes a person to go to Hell eternally?

 A. calling upon other than Allah (with *du'aa'*)
 B. murder
 C. fornication and adultery
 D. all of the above

21. How does al-Imam as-Sa'dee explain the exchange of evil deeds for good ones mentioned in Verse 70?

 A. Their sinful behavior of the past is turned into good deeds after repentance.
 B. Their sinful behavior planned for the future is fulfilled but forgiven anyway.
 C. both A and B
 D. neither A nor B

22. Regarding Verse 72 [which means]: **"And those who do not witness *zoor*..."** How does al-Imam as-Sa'dee explain **"*zoor*"**?

 A. impermissible statements and actions (in general)
 B. any speech devoid of benefit
 C. the holidays of the disbelievers
 D. all of the above

23. Which of the following is **NOT** one of the praiseworthy traits of the true worshippers of Allah indicated in Verses 63-74?

 A. They respond to ignorance with grace and restraint.
 B. They pay their *zakaat* in full.
 C. They make Hajj to the House of Allah.
 D. They supplicate to Allah alone.

24. What can be understood from Verse 77 about the supplications of the disbelievers, when they call upon Allah alone?

 A. Allah hears their supplications but does not respond to them.
 B. Allah hears their supplications and responds to them.
 C. Allah does not hear nor respond to their supplications.
 D. none of the above

25. Which of the following topics is **NOT** mentioned in *Soorah al-Furqaan*?

 A. spending moderately
 B. the revelation of the Quran
 C. angels
 D. the rightful recipients of *zakaat*

ANSWER KEY: See p.93.

APPENDIX I: SOORAH AL-FURQAAN
AND A TRANSLATION OF ITS MEANINGS

In the Name of Allah,
the Most Gracious, the Ever Merciful

بِسۡمِ ٱللَّهِ ٱلرَّحۡمَٰنِ ٱلرَّحِيمِ

1. Blessed is He Who sent down the Criterion (the Quran) to His worshipful servant, so it would be a warning to the entire creation.

تَبَارَكَ ٱلَّذِى نَزَّلَ ٱلۡفُرۡقَانَ عَلَىٰ عَبۡدِهِۦ لِيَكُونَ لِلۡعَٰلَمِينَ نَذِيرًا ۝١

2. [It is] He who possesses the dominion of the heavens and the earth; He has not begotten any son, nor does He have any partner in that dominion. And He created everything and decreed it all with precise measure.

ٱلَّذِى لَهُۥ مُلۡكُ ٱلسَّمَٰوَٰتِ وَٱلۡأَرۡضِ وَلَمۡ يَتَّخِذۡ وَلَدًا وَلَمۡ يَكُن لَّهُۥ شَرِيكٌ فِى ٱلۡمُلۡكِ وَخَلَقَ كُلَّ شَىۡءٍ فَقَدَّرَهُۥ تَقۡدِيرًا ۝٢

3. And they have taken gods besides Him; they do not create anything, whilst they are themselves created. They possess no ability to harm nor help their own selves, nor do they possess any ability to cause death, grant life, or resurrect [anyone].

وَٱتَّخَذُواْ مِن دُونِهِۦٓ ءَالِهَةً لَّا يَخۡلُقُونَ شَيۡئًا وَهُمۡ يُخۡلَقُونَ وَلَا يَمۡلِكُونَ لِأَنفُسِهِمۡ ضَرًّا وَلَا نَفۡعًا وَلَا يَمۡلِكُونَ مَوۡتًا وَلَا حَيَوٰةً وَلَا نُشُورًا ۝٣

4. Those who disbelieve have said: "This [Quran] is but a lie which he concocted, and others assisted him with that!" Indeed, they come [together] to oppress and conspire in falsehood.

وَقَالَ ٱلَّذِينَ كَفَرُوٓاْ إِنۡ هَٰذَآ إِلَّآ إِفۡكٌ ٱفۡتَرَىٰهُ وَأَعَانَهُۥ عَلَيۡهِ قَوۡمٌ ءَاخَرُونَ فَقَدۡ جَآءُو ظُلۡمًا وَزُورًا ۝٤

5. And they have said, "Myths of the ancients is what he has copied down, as they are dictated to him morning and night."

وَقَالُوٓاْ أَسَٰطِيرُ ٱلۡأَوَّلِينَ ٱكۡتَتَبَهَا فَهِىَ تُمۡلَىٰ عَلَيۡهِ بُكۡرَةً وَأَصِيلًا ۝٥

6. Say: The One who sent it down is He who knows the secrets within the heavens and earth. He is and has always been Oft-Forgiving, Ever Merciful.

قُلۡ أَنزَلَهُ ٱلَّذِى يَعۡلَمُ ٱلسِّرَّ فِى ٱلسَّمَٰوَٰتِ وَٱلۡأَرۡضِ إِنَّهُۥ كَانَ غَفُورًا رَّحِيمًا ۝٦

7. And they have said, "What is with this messenger, eating food and walking in the marketplaces? Had there only been an angel sent down to him, to be a warner along with him."

وَقَالُواْ مَالِ هَٰذَا ٱلرَّسُولِ يَأۡكُلُ ٱلطَّعَامَ وَيَمۡشِى فِى ٱلۡأَسۡوَاقِ لَوۡلَآ أُنزِلَ إِلَيۡهِ مَلَكٌ فَيَكُونَ مَعَهُۥ نَذِيرًا ۝٧

8. "Or had treasure been given to him, or if he had a garden from which he could eat." The [most] oppressive ones said, "You follow but a man under the influence of magic."

أَوْ يُلْقَىٰ إِلَيْهِ كَنْزٌ أَوْ تَكُونُ لَهُۥ جَنَّةٌ يَأْكُلُ مِنْهَا ۚ وَقَالَ ٱلظَّٰلِمُونَ إِن تَتَّبِعُونَ إِلَّا رَجُلًا مَّسْحُورًا ۝٨

9. Look at the likenesses they have put forth to describe you, [as a result] they have gone astray, and they are not able to find a way back.

ٱنظُرْ كَيْفَ ضَرَبُوا۟ لَكَ ٱلْأَمْثَٰلَ فَضَلُّوا۟ فَلَا يَسْتَطِيعُونَ سَبِيلًا ۝٩

10. Blessed is He who, if He so wills, shall grant you what is better than that: gardens under which rivers flow, and He shall make palaces for you [in Paradise].

تَبَارَكَ ٱلَّذِى إِن شَآءَ جَعَلَ لَكَ خَيْرًا مِّن ذَٰلِكَ جَنَّٰتٍ تَجْرِى مِن تَحْتِهَا ٱلْأَنْهَٰرُ وَيَجْعَل لَّكَ قُصُورًا ۝١٠

11. Yet, they reject [belief in] the Hour (the Day of Judgment). And We have prepared for those who reject the Hour a blazing fire.

بَلْ كَذَّبُوا۟ بِٱلسَّاعَةِ ۖ وَأَعْتَدْنَا لِمَن كَذَّبَ بِٱلسَّاعَةِ سَعِيرًا ۝١١

12. When it (Hell) sees them from far away, they hear its furious rage and roar.

إِذَا رَأَتْهُم مِّن مَّكَانٍ بَعِيدٍ سَمِعُوا۟ لَهَا تَغَيُّظًا وَزَفِيرًا ۝١٢

13. And when they are thrown into a crowded place within it, chained together, they wail in agony therein.

وَإِذَآ أُلْقُوا۟ مِنْهَا مَكَانًا ضَيِّقًا مُّقَرَّنِينَ دَعَوْا۟ هُنَالِكَ ثُبُورًا ۝١٣

14. Do not wail in agony only once on this day, but wail in agony many times over!

لَّا تَدْعُوا۟ ٱلْيَوْمَ ثُبُورًا وَٰحِدًا وَٱدْعُوا۟ ثُبُورًا كَثِيرًا ۝١٤

15. Say: Is that [torment] better or the Garden of Eternity promised to the pious? It will be theirs as a reward and a final destination.

قُلْ أَذَٰلِكَ خَيْرٌ أَمْ جَنَّةُ ٱلْخُلْدِ ٱلَّتِى وُعِدَ ٱلْمُتَّقُونَ ۚ كَانَتْ لَهُمْ جَزَآءً وَمَصِيرًا ۝١٥

16. They shall have therein all they desire, abiding therein forever. That is a promise from your Lord, sought from Him [alone].

لَّهُمْ فِيهَا مَا يَشَآءُونَ خَٰلِدِينَ ۚ كَانَ عَلَىٰ رَبِّكَ وَعْدًا مَّسْئُولًا ۝١٦

17. On the day when He gathers them along with what they worship besides Allah, and He says: "Was it you who misled these servants of Mine, or did they go astray from the path [on their own]?"

18. They say, "Exalted You are! It was not for us to take any protecting allies besides You, but You gave them and their fathers comfort until they forgot the reminder and became people who were ruined."

19. They have shown you to be liars for what you have said; now you have no ability to deflect [punishment away from yourselves] or to get any help. And whoever of you oppresses, We shall make him taste a severe punishment.

20. And We sent no messengers before you except that they actually ate food and walked in marketplaces. And We have made some of you as trials for others, so will you have patience? And your Lord is All-Seeing.

21. And those who do not long for the meeting with Us (i.e., disbelievers in the Day of Judgment) have said, "Had only the angels been sent down to us, or we could see our Lord!" They indeed have arrogance in their souls; they have transgressed with terrible transgressions.

22. On the day they see the angels, no glad tidings on such a day for the criminals. They (the angels) say, "Not allowed; denied!"

23. And We turn to whatever deeds they did, and We make that into scattered dust.

وَيَوْمَ يَحْشُرُهُمْ وَمَا يَعْبُدُونَ مِن دُونِ ٱللَّهِ فَيَقُولُ ءَأَنتُمْ أَضْلَلْتُمْ عِبَادِى هَـٰٓؤُلَآءِ أَمْ هُمْ ضَلُّوا۟ ٱلسَّبِيلَ ﴿١٧﴾

قَالُوا۟ سُبْحَـٰنَكَ مَا كَانَ يَنۢبَغِى لَنَآ أَن نَّتَّخِذَ مِن دُونِكَ مِنْ أَوْلِيَآءَ وَلَـٰكِن مَّتَّعْتَهُمْ وَءَابَآءَهُمْ حَتَّىٰ نَسُوا۟ ٱلذِّكْرَ وَكَانُوا۟ قَوْمًۢا بُورًا ﴿١٨﴾

فَقَدْ كَذَّبُوكُم بِمَا تَقُولُونَ فَمَا تَسْتَطِيعُونَ صَرْفًا وَلَا نَصْرًا وَمَن يَظْلِم مِّنكُمْ نُذِقْهُ عَذَابًا كَبِيرًا ﴿١٩﴾

وَمَآ أَرْسَلْنَا قَبْلَكَ مِنَ ٱلْمُرْسَلِينَ إِلَّآ إِنَّهُمْ لَيَأْكُلُونَ ٱلطَّعَامَ وَيَمْشُونَ فِى ٱلْأَسْوَاقِ وَجَعَلْنَا بَعْضَكُمْ لِبَعْضٍ فِتْنَةً أَتَصْبِرُونَ وَكَانَ رَبُّكَ بَصِيرًا ﴿٢٠﴾

وَقَالَ ٱلَّذِينَ لَا يَرْجُونَ لِقَآءَنَا لَوْلَآ أُنزِلَ عَلَيْنَا ٱلْمَلَـٰٓئِكَةُ أَوْ نَرَىٰ رَبَّنَا لَقَدِ ٱسْتَكْبَرُوا۟ فِىٓ أَنفُسِهِمْ وَعَتَوْ عُتُوًّا كَبِيرًا ﴿٢١﴾

يَوْمَ يَرَوْنَ ٱلْمَلَـٰٓئِكَةَ لَا بُشْرَىٰ يَوْمَئِذٍ لِّلْمُجْرِمِينَ وَيَقُولُونَ حِجْرًا مَّحْجُورًا ﴿٢٢﴾

وَقَدِمْنَآ إِلَىٰ مَا عَمِلُوا۟ مِنْ عَمَلٍ فَجَعَلْنَـٰهُ هَبَآءً مَّنثُورًا ﴿٢٣﴾

24. The residents of Paradise on that day have better abodes and finer places of relaxation.

25. The day when the sky cracks apart with clouds, and the angels are made to descend, an undeniably real descending.

26. All sovereignty on that day is rightfully owned by the Most Gracious (Allah alone); for the disbelievers it is a day of difficulty.

27. The day when the wrongdoer bites at his hands, saying, "I wish I would have taken a path following along with the Messenger!"

28. "O woe to me! I wish I had never taken So-and-So as a close friend!"

29. "He did indeed lead me astray from the Reminder (the Quran) after it had come to me." The devil continues to betray and desert people.

30. And the Messenger says: "O my Lord! My people have indeed abandoned this Quran."

31. Thus We assign to every prophet an enemy among the criminals, whilst your Lord suffices as a Guide and a Helper.

32. And those who disbelieve have said: "Had only the Quran been sent down to him all at once!" Like that [it was revealed in stages], so We would make your heart firm with it. And We have revealed it gradually, in stages.

33. And they bring you no parable except that We bring you the Truth [about that matter] and a better explanation of it.

أَصْحَٰبُ ٱلْجَنَّةِ يَوْمَئِذٍ خَيْرٌ مُّسْتَقَرًّا وَأَحْسَنُ مَقِيلًا ﴿٢٤﴾

وَيَوْمَ تَشَقَّقُ ٱلسَّمَآءُ بِٱلْغَمَٰمِ وَنُزِّلَ ٱلْمَلَٰٓئِكَةُ تَنزِيلًا ﴿٢٥﴾

ٱلْمُلْكُ يَوْمَئِذٍ ٱلْحَقُّ لِلرَّحْمَٰنِ ۚ وَكَانَ يَوْمًا عَلَى ٱلْكَٰفِرِينَ عَسِيرًا ﴿٢٦﴾

وَيَوْمَ يَعَضُّ ٱلظَّالِمُ عَلَىٰ يَدَيْهِ يَقُولُ يَٰلَيْتَنِى ٱتَّخَذْتُ مَعَ ٱلرَّسُولِ سَبِيلًا ﴿٢٧﴾

يَٰوَيْلَتَىٰ لَيْتَنِى لَمْ أَتَّخِذْ فُلَانًا خَلِيلًا ﴿٢٨﴾

لَّقَدْ أَضَلَّنِى عَنِ ٱلذِّكْرِ بَعْدَ إِذْ جَآءَنِى ۗ وَكَانَ ٱلشَّيْطَٰنُ لِلْإِنسَٰنِ خَذُولًا ﴿٢٩﴾

وَقَالَ ٱلرَّسُولُ يَٰرَبِّ إِنَّ قَوْمِى ٱتَّخَذُوا۟ هَٰذَا ٱلْقُرْءَانَ مَهْجُورًا ﴿٣٠﴾

وَكَذَٰلِكَ جَعَلْنَا لِكُلِّ نَبِىٍّ عَدُوًّا مِّنَ ٱلْمُجْرِمِينَ ۗ وَكَفَىٰ بِرَبِّكَ هَادِيًا وَنَصِيرًا ﴿٣١﴾

وَقَالَ ٱلَّذِينَ كَفَرُوا۟ لَوْلَا نُزِّلَ عَلَيْهِ ٱلْقُرْءَانُ جُمْلَةً وَٰحِدَةً ۚ كَذَٰلِكَ لِنُثَبِّتَ بِهِۦ فُؤَادَكَ ۖ وَرَتَّلْنَٰهُ تَرْتِيلًا ﴿٣٢﴾

وَلَا يَأْتُونَكَ بِمَثَلٍ إِلَّا جِئْنَٰكَ بِٱلْحَقِّ وَأَحْسَنَ تَفْسِيرًا ﴿٣٣﴾

34. Those gathered upon their faces unto Jahannam, such are in a worse place, [upon] a more misguided path.

35. And indeed We gave Moosaa (Moses) the Book and appointed his brother, Haaroon (Aaron), as a helper for him.

36. And We said: "Go to the people who have disbelieved in Our aayaat (signs and verses)." Then, We destroyed them with utter destruction.

37. And Nooh's (Noah's) people, when they disbelieved in the messengers, We drowned them; We made them a lesson of guidance for all humankind. And We have prepared a painful punishment for the wrong doers.

38. And [the civilizations of] 'Aad and Thamood, as well as the people of [the Well of] Ar-Rass, including many generations between those.

39. For each [of them] We provided examples [to guide them], yet each [of them] We annihilated with absolute destruction.

40. And indeed they have come to the town which had evil rain poured down upon it. Did they not even see it [themselves, firsthand]? Yet they [still] would not hope for any resurrection.

41. And when they see you, they only take you as a joke, [saying]: "Is this the one whom Allah has sent as a Messenger?"

42. "He would have nearly misled us away from our gods, had it not been that we were steadfast [in our worship of them]!" And they will come to know when they see the punishment, who is most misguided!

ٱلَّذِينَ يُحْشَرُونَ عَلَىٰ وُجُوهِهِمْ إِلَىٰ جَهَنَّمَ أُوْلَـٰٓئِكَ شَرٌّ مَّكَانًا وَأَضَلُّ سَبِيلًا ﴿٣٤﴾

وَلَقَدْ ءَاتَيْنَا مُوسَى ٱلْكِتَـٰبَ وَجَعَلْنَا مَعَهُۥٓ أَخَاهُ هَـٰرُونَ وَزِيرًا ﴿٣٥﴾

فَقُلْنَا ٱذْهَبَآ إِلَى ٱلْقَوْمِ ٱلَّذِينَ كَذَّبُوا۟ بِـَٔايَـٰتِنَا فَدَمَّرْنَـٰهُمْ تَدْمِيرًا ﴿٣٦﴾

وَقَوْمَ نُوحٍ لَّمَّا كَذَّبُوا۟ ٱلرُّسُلَ أَغْرَقْنَـٰهُمْ وَجَعَلْنَـٰهُمْ لِلنَّاسِ ءَايَةً وَأَعْتَدْنَا لِلظَّـٰلِمِينَ عَذَابًا أَلِيمًا ﴿٣٧﴾

وَعَادًا وَثَمُودَا۟ وَأَصْحَـٰبَ ٱلرَّسِّ وَقُرُونًا بَيْنَ ذَٰلِكَ كَثِيرًا ﴿٣٨﴾

وَكُلًّا ضَرَبْنَا لَهُ ٱلْأَمْثَـٰلَ ۖ وَكُلًّا تَبَّرْنَا تَتْبِيرًا ﴿٣٩﴾

وَلَقَدْ أَتَوْا۟ عَلَى ٱلْقَرْيَةِ ٱلَّتِىٓ أُمْطِرَتْ مَطَرَ ٱلسَّوْءِ أَفَلَمْ يَكُونُوا۟ يَرَوْنَهَا ۚ بَلْ كَانُوا۟ لَا يَرْجُونَ نُشُورًا ﴿٤٠﴾

وَإِذَا رَأَوْكَ إِن يَتَّخِذُونَكَ إِلَّا هُزُوًا أَهَـٰذَا ٱلَّذِى بَعَثَ ٱللَّهُ رَسُولًا ﴿٤١﴾

إِن كَادَ لَيُضِلُّنَا عَنْ ءَالِهَتِنَا لَوْلَآ أَن صَبَرْنَا عَلَيْهَا ۚ وَسَوْفَ يَعْلَمُونَ حِينَ يَرَوْنَ ٱلْعَذَابَ مَنْ أَضَلُّ سَبِيلًا ﴿٤٢﴾

43. Have you seen him who has taken his own whims as his god? Could you then be responsible for him?

44. Or do you assume that most of them [actually] listen or comprehend? They are only like cattle, or yet even further astray [than cattle]!

45. Have you not seen how your Lord extends the shadow? Had He willed, He would have made it still. Then, We have made the sun its guide.

46. Then, We bring it back unto Us in gradual withdrawal.

47. And He is the One who has made the night a covering for you and sleep as relaxation, and He has made the daytime [for you to] spread out.

48. And He is the One who has sent the winds as favorable signs of His imminent Mercy (i.e., the rain). And We have sent down clean [and purifying] water from the sky,

49. So that We give life by it to dead land, and We provide drink from it to what We have created of cattle and so many people.

50. And indeed We have distributed it amongst them so they might be reminded, but most people refuse to be anything but ingrates.

51. And had We so willed, We would have sent a warner to every town.

52. So do not obey the disbelievers; instead engage them with it (the Quran), with great efforts [in propagating Islam].

أَرَءَيْتَ مَنِ ٱتَّخَذَ إِلَٰهَهُۥ هَوَىٰهُ أَفَأَنتَ تَكُونُ عَلَيْهِ وَكِيلًا ﴿٤٣﴾

أَمْ تَحْسَبُ أَنَّ أَكْثَرَهُمْ يَسْمَعُونَ أَوْ يَعْقِلُونَ إِنْ هُمْ إِلَّا كَٱلْأَنْعَٰمِ بَلْ هُمْ أَضَلُّ سَبِيلًا ﴿٤٤﴾

أَلَمْ تَرَ إِلَىٰ رَبِّكَ كَيْفَ مَدَّ ٱلظِّلَّ وَلَوْ شَآءَ لَجَعَلَهُۥ سَاكِنًا ثُمَّ جَعَلْنَا ٱلشَّمْسَ عَلَيْهِ دَلِيلًا ﴿٤٥﴾

ثُمَّ قَبَضْنَٰهُ إِلَيْنَا قَبْضًا يَسِيرًا ﴿٤٦﴾

وَهُوَ ٱلَّذِى جَعَلَ لَكُمُ ٱلَّيْلَ لِبَاسًا وَٱلنَّوْمَ سُبَاتًا وَجَعَلَ ٱلنَّهَارَ نُشُورًا ﴿٤٧﴾

وَهُوَ ٱلَّذِىٓ أَرْسَلَ ٱلرِّيَٰحَ بُشْرًۢا بَيْنَ يَدَىْ رَحْمَتِهِۦ وَأَنزَلْنَا مِنَ ٱلسَّمَآءِ مَآءً طَهُورًا ﴿٤٨﴾

لِّنُحْۦِىَ بِهِۦ بَلْدَةً مَّيْتًا وَنُسْقِيَهُۥ مِمَّا خَلَقْنَآ أَنْعَٰمًا وَأَنَاسِىَّ كَثِيرًا ﴿٤٩﴾

وَلَقَدْ صَرَّفْنَٰهُ بَيْنَهُمْ لِيَذَّكَّرُوا۟ فَأَبَىٰٓ أَكْثَرُ ٱلنَّاسِ إِلَّا كُفُورًا ﴿٥٠﴾

وَلَوْ شِئْنَا لَبَعَثْنَا فِى كُلِّ قَرْيَةٍ نَّذِيرًا ﴿٥١﴾

فَلَا تُطِعِ ٱلْكَٰفِرِينَ وَجَٰهِدْهُم بِهِۦ جِهَادًا كَبِيرًا ﴿٥٢﴾

53. And He is the One who has released both bodies of water; this one is sweet and palatable, and the other is salty and bitter. And He has made a barrier and a fortified partition between them.

54. And He is the One who created humankind from water, and He has made relatives for him through blood lineage and marriage. And your Lord is All-Capable.

55. And yet they worship others besides Allah, things which cannot help them nor harm them! The disbeliever is ever supportive [of falsehood] in opposition to your Lord.

56. And We have only sent you as a herald of glad tidings and a warner.

57. Say: I do not ask you for any compensation for this, yet one may choose to take a path unto His Lord.

58. And place your trust in the Ever Living who never dies, and glorify His praises. Sufficient is He as One Ever Aware of the sins of His slaves.

59. The One who created the heavens and the earth, including all that is between them, in six days. Then, He ascended above the throne. The Most Gracious, ask One who is All-Aware about Him[self].

60. And when it is said to them, "Prostrate unto the Most Gracious," they say, "And what is the Most Gracious? Shall we just prostrate unto whatever you command us?" Such only increases them in aversion.

61. Blessed is He Who placed within the heavens constellations, and He placed therein a lamp and a moon shining with light.

62. And He is the One who has put the night and the day in succession, for anyone who wants to be reminded or wants [to show] gratitude.

وَهُوَ ٱلَّذِى مَرَجَ ٱلْبَحْرَيْنِ هَٰذَا عَذْبٌ فُرَاتٌ وَهَٰذَا مِلْحٌ أُجَاجٌ وَجَعَلَ بَيْنَهُمَا بَرْزَخًا وَحِجْرًا مَّحْجُورًا ۝

وَهُوَ ٱلَّذِى خَلَقَ مِنَ ٱلْمَآءِ بَشَرًا فَجَعَلَهُۥ نَسَبًا وَصِهْرًا ۗ وَكَانَ رَبُّكَ قَدِيرًا ۝

وَيَعْبُدُونَ مِن دُونِ ٱللَّهِ مَا لَا يَنفَعُهُمْ وَلَا يَضُرُّهُمْ ۗ وَكَانَ ٱلْكَافِرُ عَلَىٰ رَبِّهِۦ ظَهِيرًا ۝

وَمَآ أَرْسَلْنَٰكَ إِلَّا مُبَشِّرًا وَنَذِيرًا ۝

قُلْ مَآ أَسْـَٔلُكُمْ عَلَيْهِ مِنْ أَجْرٍ إِلَّا مَن شَآءَ أَن يَتَّخِذَ إِلَىٰ رَبِّهِۦ سَبِيلًا ۝

وَتَوَكَّلْ عَلَى ٱلْحَىِّ ٱلَّذِى لَا يَمُوتُ وَسَبِّحْ بِحَمْدِهِۦ ۚ وَكَفَىٰ بِهِۦ بِذُنُوبِ عِبَادِهِۦ خَبِيرًا ۝

ٱلَّذِى خَلَقَ ٱلسَّمَٰوَٰتِ وَٱلْأَرْضَ وَمَا بَيْنَهُمَا فِى سِتَّةِ أَيَّامٍ ثُمَّ ٱسْتَوَىٰ عَلَى ٱلْعَرْشِ ۚ ٱلرَّحْمَٰنُ فَسْـَٔلْ بِهِۦ خَبِيرًا ۝

وَإِذَا قِيلَ لَهُمُ ٱسْجُدُوا۟ لِلرَّحْمَٰنِ قَالُوا۟ وَمَا ٱلرَّحْمَٰنُ أَنَسْجُدُ لِمَا تَأْمُرُنَا وَزَادَهُمْ نُفُورًا ۩ ۝

تَبَارَكَ ٱلَّذِى جَعَلَ فِى ٱلسَّمَآءِ بُرُوجًا وَجَعَلَ فِيهَا سِرَٰجًا وَقَمَرًا مُّنِيرًا ۝

وَهُوَ ٱلَّذِى جَعَلَ ٱلَّيْلَ وَٱلنَّهَارَ خِلْفَةً لِّمَنْ أَرَادَ أَن يَذَّكَّرَ أَوْ أَرَادَ شُكُورًا ۝

63. And the [real] worshippers of the Most Gracious are those who walk the land in humble serenity, and when the foolish address them, they respond with innocent words [keeping them safe from sin].

64. And those who spend the night focused on their Lord, prostrating and standing [in prayer].

65. And those who say: "Our Lord! Keep the punishment of Jahannam from us!" Its punishment is indeed an ongoing penalty.

66. What a terrible abode and place to dwell that is!

67. And when they spend, they are neither extravagant nor miserly, but they take a middle course between those [extremes].

68. And those who do not call upon any other deity along with Allah, nor do they take any life which Allah has forbidden, except with just cause, nor do they fornicate. Whoever does that shall encounter punishment for sin!

69. The punishment will be multiplied on him on the Day of Resurrection; he will abide therein in disgrace.

70. But not those who repent, believe, and do righteous deeds, for such people, Allah replaces their sins with good deeds, and Allah is Oft-Forgiving, Ever Merciful.

71. And whoever repents and does righteous deeds, then he truly repents unto Allah with genuine repentance.

72. And [they are] those who do not witness falsehood, and if they [even] pass by some frivolity, they pass by with dignity.

وَعِبَادُ ٱلرَّحْمَٰنِ ٱلَّذِينَ يَمْشُونَ عَلَى ٱلْأَرْضِ هَوْنًا وَإِذَا خَاطَبَهُمُ ٱلْجَٰهِلُونَ قَالُوا۟ سَلَٰمًا ﴿٦٣﴾

وَٱلَّذِينَ يَبِيتُونَ لِرَبِّهِمْ سُجَّدًا وَقِيَٰمًا ﴿٦٤﴾

وَٱلَّذِينَ يَقُولُونَ رَبَّنَا ٱصْرِفْ عَنَّا عَذَابَ جَهَنَّمَ إِنَّ عَذَابَهَا كَانَ غَرَامًا ﴿٦٥﴾

إِنَّهَا سَآءَتْ مُسْتَقَرًّا وَمُقَامًا ﴿٦٦﴾

وَٱلَّذِينَ إِذَآ أَنفَقُوا۟ لَمْ يُسْرِفُوا۟ وَلَمْ يَقْتُرُوا۟ وَكَانَ بَيْنَ ذَٰلِكَ قَوَامًا ﴿٦٧﴾

وَٱلَّذِينَ لَا يَدْعُونَ مَعَ ٱللَّهِ إِلَٰهًا ءَاخَرَ وَلَا يَقْتُلُونَ ٱلنَّفْسَ ٱلَّتِى حَرَّمَ ٱللَّهُ إِلَّا بِٱلْحَقِّ وَلَا يَزْنُونَ وَمَن يَفْعَلْ ذَٰلِكَ يَلْقَ أَثَامًا ﴿٦٨﴾

يُضَٰعَفْ لَهُ ٱلْعَذَابُ يَوْمَ ٱلْقِيَٰمَةِ وَيَخْلُدْ فِيهِۦ مُهَانًا ﴿٦٩﴾

إِلَّا مَن تَابَ وَءَامَنَ وَعَمِلَ عَمَلًا صَٰلِحًا فَأُو۟لَٰٓئِكَ يُبَدِّلُ ٱللَّهُ سَيِّـَٔاتِهِمْ حَسَنَٰتٍ وَكَانَ ٱللَّهُ غَفُورًا رَّحِيمًا ﴿٧٠﴾

وَمَن تَابَ وَعَمِلَ صَٰلِحًا فَإِنَّهُۥ يَتُوبُ إِلَى ٱللَّهِ مَتَابًا ﴿٧١﴾

وَٱلَّذِينَ لَا يَشْهَدُونَ ٱلزُّورَ وَإِذَا مَرُّوا۟ بِٱللَّغْوِ مَرُّوا۟ كِرَامًا ﴿٧٢﴾

73. And [they are] those who, when reminded of the aayaat (signs and Verses) of their Lord, they do not turn away from that, [pretending to be] deaf and blind.

74. And [they are] those who say, "Our Lord, give us among our mates and offspring what will be a comfort to our eyes, and make us leading examples for the pious."

75. Such are rewarded with lofty abodes [in Paradise], a result of their patience. They are met therein with greetings and safety.

76. Abiding therein forever; what a fine abode and place to dwell!

77. Say: My Lord would have paid you no attention, had it not been for your supplications [to Him]. Yet you have indeed rejected [the truth], and so it shall be never-ending punishment.

وَٱلَّذِينَ إِذَا ذُكِّرُواْ بِآيَٰتِ رَبِّهِمْ لَمْ يَخِرُّواْ عَلَيْهَا صُمًّا وَعُمْيَانًا ۝٧٣

وَٱلَّذِينَ يَقُولُونَ رَبَّنَا هَبْ لَنَا مِنْ أَزْوَٰجِنَا وَذُرِّيَّٰتِنَا قُرَّةَ أَعْيُنٍ وَٱجْعَلْنَا لِلْمُتَّقِينَ إِمَامًا ۝٧٤

أُوْلَٰئِكَ يُجْزَوْنَ ٱلْغُرْفَةَ بِمَا صَبَرُواْ وَيُلَقَّوْنَ فِيهَا تَحِيَّةً وَسَلَٰمًا ۝٧٥

خَٰلِدِينَ فِيهَا حَسُنَتْ مُسْتَقَرًّا وَمُقَامًا ۝٧٦

قُلْ مَا يَعْبَؤُاْ بِكُمْ رَبِّي لَوْلَا دُعَآؤُكُمْ فَقَدْ كَذَّبْتُمْ فَسَوْفَ يَكُونُ لِزَامًا ۝٧٧

ANSWER KEY TO THE MULTIPLE CHOICE QUIZZES & FINAL EXAM

	QUIZ 1	QUIZ 2	QUIZ 3	QUIZ 4	QUIZ 5	
	1. C	1. C	1. C	1. C	11. A	21. A
	2. D	2. C	2. D	2. D	12. C	22. A
	3. B	3. D	3. B	3. A	13. D	23. C
	4. A	4. D	4. A	4. B	14. B	24. B
	5. D	5. B	5. D	5. A	15. D	25. D
	6. B	6. C	6. B	6. A	6. C	16. A
	7. A	7. C	7. A	7. A	7. A	17. A
	8. D	8. A	8. A	8. C	8. C	18. B
	9. C	9. C	9. A	9. A	9. C	19. D
	10. B	10. B	10. B	10. B	10. C	20. A

Printed in Great Britain
by Amazon

39568816R00057

إِنَّمَا الْمُؤْمِنُونَ الَّذِينَ ءَامَنُوا بِاللَّهِ وَرَسُولِهِ وَإِذَا كَانُوا مَعَهُ

عَلَىٰ أَمْرٍ جَامِعٍ لَّمْ يَذْهَبُوا حَتَّىٰ يَسْتَـْٔذِنُوهُ إِنَّ الَّذِينَ يَسْتَـْٔذِنُونَكَ

أُولَـٰئِكَ الَّذِينَ يُؤْمِنُونَ بِاللَّهِ وَرَسُولِهِ فَإِذَا اسْتَـْٔذَنُوكَ

لِبَعْضِ شَأْنِهِمْ فَأْذَن لِّمَن شِئْتَ مِنْهُمْ وَاسْتَغْفِرْ لَهُمُ

اللَّهَ إِنَّ اللَّهَ غَفُورٌ رَّحِيمٌ ۝ لَّا تَجْعَلُوا دُعَاءَ الرَّسُولِ

بَيْنَكُمْ كَدُعَاءِ بَعْضِكُم بَعْضًا قَدْ يَعْلَمُ اللَّهُ الَّذِينَ

يَتَسَلَّلُونَ مِنكُمْ لِوَاذًا فَلْيَحْذَرِ الَّذِينَ يُخَالِفُونَ عَنْ

أَمْرِهِ أَن تُصِيبَهُمْ فِتْنَةٌ أَوْ يُصِيبَهُمْ عَذَابٌ أَلِيمٌ ۝ أَلَا إِنَّ

لِلَّهِ مَا فِي السَّمَـٰوَاتِ وَالْأَرْضِ قَدْ يَعْلَمُ مَا أَنتُمْ عَلَيْهِ وَيَوْمَ

يُرْجَعُونَ إِلَيْهِ فَيُنَبِّئُهُم بِمَا عَمِلُوا وَاللَّهُ بِكُلِّ شَيْءٍ عَلِيمٌ ۝

سُورَةُ الْفُرْقَانِ

بِسْمِ اللَّهِ الرَّحْمَـٰنِ الرَّحِيمِ

تَبَارَكَ الَّذِي نَزَّلَ الْفُرْقَانَ عَلَىٰ عَبْدِهِ لِيَكُونَ لِلْعَالَمِينَ نَذِيرًا

۝ الَّذِي لَهُ مُلْكُ السَّمَـٰوَاتِ وَالْأَرْضِ وَلَمْ يَتَّخِذْ وَلَدًا وَلَمْ يَكُن

لَّهُ شَرِيكٌ فِي الْمُلْكِ وَخَلَقَ كُلَّ شَيْءٍ فَقَدَّرَهُ تَقْدِيرًا ۝

وَاتَّخَذُوا مِن دُونِهِۦٓ ءَالِهَةً لَّا يَخْلُقُونَ شَيْـًٔا وَهُمْ يُخْلَقُونَ وَلَا يَمْلِكُونَ لِأَنفُسِهِمْ ضَرًّا وَلَا نَفْعًا وَلَا يَمْلِكُونَ مَوْتًا وَلَا حَيَوٰةً وَلَا نُشُورًا ۝٣ وَقَالَ ٱلَّذِينَ كَفَرُوٓا إِنْ هَٰذَآ إِلَّآ إِفْكٌ ٱفْتَرَىٰهُ وَأَعَانَهُۥ عَلَيْهِ قَوْمٌ ءَاخَرُونَ فَقَدْ جَآءُو ظُلْمًا وَزُورًا ۝٤ وَقَالُوٓا أَسَٰطِيرُ ٱلْأَوَّلِينَ ٱكْتَتَبَهَا فَهِيَ تُمْلَىٰ عَلَيْهِ بُكْرَةً وَأَصِيلًا ۝٥ قُلْ أَنزَلَهُ ٱلَّذِي يَعْلَمُ ٱلسِّرَّ فِي ٱلسَّمَٰوَٰتِ وَٱلْأَرْضِ إِنَّهُۥ كَانَ غَفُورًا رَّحِيمًا ۝٦ وَقَالُوا مَالِ هَٰذَا ٱلرَّسُولِ يَأْكُلُ ٱلطَّعَامَ وَيَمْشِي فِي ٱلْأَسْوَاقِ لَوْلَآ أُنزِلَ إِلَيْهِ مَلَكٌ فَيَكُونَ مَعَهُۥ نَذِيرًا ۝٧ أَوْ يُلْقَىٰٓ إِلَيْهِ كَنزٌ أَوْ تَكُونُ لَهُۥ جَنَّةٌ يَأْكُلُ مِنْهَا وَقَالَ ٱلظَّٰلِمُونَ إِن تَتَّبِعُونَ إِلَّا رَجُلًا مَّسْحُورًا ۝٨ ٱنظُرْ كَيْفَ ضَرَبُوا لَكَ ٱلْأَمْثَٰلَ فَضَلُّوا فَلَا يَسْتَطِيعُونَ سَبِيلًا ۝٩ تَبَارَكَ ٱلَّذِيٓ إِن شَآءَ جَعَلَ لَكَ خَيْرًا مِّن ذَٰلِكَ جَنَّٰتٍ تَجْرِي مِن تَحْتِهَا ٱلْأَنْهَٰرُ وَيَجْعَل لَّكَ قُصُورًا ۝١٠ بَلْ كَذَّبُوا بِٱلسَّاعَةِ وَأَعْتَدْنَا لِمَن كَذَّبَ بِٱلسَّاعَةِ سَعِيرًا ۝١١

إِذَا رَأَتْهُم مِّن مَّكَانٍ بَعِيدٍ سَمِعُوا لَهَا تَغَيُّظًا وَزَفِيرًا ﴿١٢﴾

وَإِذَآ أُلْقُوا مِنْهَا مَكَانًا ضَيِّقًا مُّقَرَّنِينَ دَعَوْا هُنَالِكَ ثُبُورًا

﴿١٣﴾ لَّا تَدْعُوا الْيَوْمَ ثُبُورًا وَاحِدًا وَادْعُوا ثُبُورًا كَثِيرًا ﴿١٤﴾

قُلْ أَذَٰلِكَ خَيْرٌ أَمْ جَنَّةُ الْخُلْدِ الَّتِي وُعِدَ الْمُتَّقُونَ كَانَتْ

لَهُمْ جَزَآءً وَمَصِيرًا ﴿١٥﴾ لَّهُمْ فِيهَا مَا يَشَآءُونَ خَالِدِينَ

كَانَ عَلَىٰ رَبِّكَ وَعْدًا مَّسْئُولًا ﴿١٦﴾ وَيَوْمَ يَحْشُرُهُمْ وَمَا

يَعْبُدُونَ مِن دُونِ اللَّهِ فَيَقُولُ ءَأَنتُمْ أَضْلَلْتُمْ عِبَادِي

هَٰؤُلَآءِ أَمْ هُمْ ضَلُّوا السَّبِيلَ ﴿١٧﴾ قَالُوا سُبْحَانَكَ مَا كَانَ

يَنبَغِي لَنَآ أَن نَّتَّخِذَ مِن دُونِكَ مِنْ أَوْلِيَآءَ وَلَٰكِن مَّتَّعْتَهُمْ

وَءَابَآءَهُمْ حَتَّىٰ نَسُوا الذِّكْرَ وَكَانُوا قَوْمًا بُورًا ﴿١٨﴾

فَقَدْ كَذَّبُوكُم بِمَا تَقُولُونَ فَمَا تَسْتَطِيعُونَ صَرْفًا

وَلَا نَصْرًا وَمَن يَظْلِم مِّنكُمْ نُذِقْهُ عَذَابًا كَبِيرًا ﴿١٩﴾

وَمَآ أَرْسَلْنَا قَبْلَكَ مِنَ الْمُرْسَلِينَ إِلَّا إِنَّهُمْ لَيَأْكُلُونَ

الطَّعَامَ وَيَمْشُونَ فِي الْأَسْوَاقِ وَجَعَلْنَا بَعْضَكُمْ

لِبَعْضٍ فِتْنَةً أَتَصْبِرُونَ وَكَانَ رَبُّكَ بَصِيرًا ﴿٢٠﴾

۞ وَقَالَ الَّذِينَ لَا يَرْجُونَ لِقَاءَنَا لَوْلَا أُنزِلَ عَلَيْنَا الْمَلَٰئِكَةُ أَوْ نَرَىٰ رَبَّنَا لَقَدِ اسْتَكْبَرُوا فِىٓ أَنفُسِهِمْ وَعَتَوْ عُتُوًّا كَبِيرًا ﴿٢١﴾ يَوْمَ يَرَوْنَ الْمَلَٰئِكَةَ لَا بُشْرَىٰ يَوْمَئِذٍ لِّلْمُجْرِمِينَ وَيَقُولُونَ حِجْرًا مَّحْجُورًا ﴿٢٢﴾ وَقَدِمْنَآ إِلَىٰ مَا عَمِلُوا مِنْ عَمَلٍ فَجَعَلْنَٰهُ هَبَآءً مَّنثُورًا ﴿٢٣﴾ أَصْحَٰبُ الْجَنَّةِ يَوْمَئِذٍ خَيْرٌ مُّسْتَقَرًّا وَأَحْسَنُ مَقِيلًا ﴿٢٤﴾ وَيَوْمَ تَشَقَّقُ السَّمَآءُ بِالْغَمَٰمِ وَنُزِّلَ الْمَلَٰئِكَةُ تَنزِيلًا ﴿٢٥﴾ الْمُلْكُ يَوْمَئِذٍ الْحَقُّ لِلرَّحْمَٰنِ وَكَانَ يَوْمًا عَلَى الْكَٰفِرِينَ عَسِيرًا ﴿٢٦﴾ وَيَوْمَ يَعَضُّ الظَّالِمُ عَلَىٰ يَدَيْهِ يَقُولُ يَٰلَيْتَنِى اتَّخَذْتُ مَعَ الرَّسُولِ سَبِيلًا ﴿٢٧﴾ يَٰوَيْلَتَىٰ لَيْتَنِى لَمْ أَتَّخِذْ فُلَانًا خَلِيلًا ﴿٢٨﴾ لَّقَدْ أَضَلَّنِى عَنِ الذِّكْرِ بَعْدَ إِذْ جَآءَنِى وَكَانَ الشَّيْطَٰنُ لِلْإِنسَٰنِ خَذُولًا ﴿٢٩﴾ وَقَالَ الرَّسُولُ يَٰرَبِّ إِنَّ قَوْمِى اتَّخَذُوا هَٰذَا الْقُرْءَانَ مَهْجُورًا ﴿٣٠﴾ وَكَذَٰلِكَ جَعَلْنَا لِكُلِّ نَبِىٍّ عَدُوًّا مِّنَ الْمُجْرِمِينَ وَكَفَىٰ بِرَبِّكَ هَادِيًا وَنَصِيرًا ﴿٣١﴾ وَقَالَ الَّذِينَ كَفَرُوا لَوْلَا نُزِّلَ عَلَيْهِ الْقُرْءَانُ جُمْلَةً وَٰحِدَةً كَذَٰلِكَ لِنُثَبِّتَ بِهِ فُؤَادَكَ وَرَتَّلْنَٰهُ تَرْتِيلًا ﴿٣٢﴾

وَلَا يَأْتُونَكَ بِمَثَلٍ إِلَّا جِئْنَـٰكَ بِٱلْحَقِّ وَأَحْسَنَ تَفْسِيرًا ۝٣٣ ٱلَّذِينَ يُحْشَرُونَ عَلَىٰ وُجُوهِهِمْ إِلَىٰ جَهَنَّمَ أُوْلَـٰٓئِكَ شَرٌّ مَّكَانًا وَأَضَلُّ سَبِيلًا ۝٣٤ وَلَقَدْ ءَاتَيْنَا مُوسَى ٱلْكِتَـٰبَ وَجَعَلْنَا مَعَهُۥٓ أَخَاهُ هَـٰرُونَ وَزِيرًا ۝٣٥ فَقُلْنَا ٱذْهَبَآ إِلَى ٱلْقَوْمِ ٱلَّذِينَ كَذَّبُواْ بِـَٔايَـٰتِنَا فَدَمَّرْنَـٰهُمْ تَدْمِيرًا ۝٣٦ وَقَوْمَ نُوحٍ لَّمَّا كَذَّبُواْ ٱلرُّسُلَ أَغْرَقْنَـٰهُمْ وَجَعَلْنَـٰهُمْ لِلنَّاسِ ءَايَةً وَأَعْتَدْنَا لِلظَّـٰلِمِينَ عَذَابًا أَلِيمًا ۝٣٧ وَعَادًا وَثَمُودَاْ وَأَصْحَـٰبَ ٱلرَّسِّ وَقُرُونًا بَيْنَ ذَٰلِكَ كَثِيرًا ۝٣٨ وَكُلًّا ضَرَبْنَا لَهُ ٱلْأَمْثَـٰلَ وَكُلًّا تَبَّرْنَا تَتْبِيرًا ۝٣٩ وَلَقَدْ أَتَوْاْ عَلَى ٱلْقَرْيَةِ ٱلَّتِىٓ أُمْطِرَتْ مَطَرَ ٱلسَّوْءِ أَفَلَمْ يَكُونُواْ يَرَوْنَهَا بَلْ كَانُواْ لَا يَرْجُونَ نُشُورًا ۝٤٠ وَإِذَا رَأَوْكَ إِن يَتَّخِذُونَكَ إِلَّا هُزُوًا أَهَـٰذَا ٱلَّذِى بَعَثَ ٱللَّهُ رَسُولًا ۝٤١ إِن كَادَ لَيُضِلُّنَا عَنْ ءَالِهَتِنَا لَوْلَآ أَن صَبَرْنَا عَلَيْهَا وَسَوْفَ يَعْلَمُونَ حِينَ يَرَوْنَ ٱلْعَذَابَ مَنْ أَضَلُّ سَبِيلًا ۝٤٢ أَرَءَيْتَ مَنِ ٱتَّخَذَ إِلَـٰهَهُۥ هَوَىٰهُ أَفَأَنتَ تَكُونُ عَلَيْهِ وَكِيلًا ۝٤٣

أَمْ تَحْسَبُ أَنَّ أَكْثَرَهُمْ يَسْمَعُونَ أَوْ يَعْقِلُونَ ۚ إِنْ هُمْ إِلَّا كَالْأَنْعَامِ ۖ بَلْ هُمْ أَضَلُّ سَبِيلًا ﴿٤٤﴾ أَلَمْ تَرَ إِلَىٰ رَبِّكَ كَيْفَ مَدَّ الظِّلَّ وَلَوْ شَاءَ لَجَعَلَهُ سَاكِنًا ثُمَّ جَعَلْنَا الشَّمْسَ عَلَيْهِ دَلِيلًا ﴿٤٥﴾ ثُمَّ قَبَضْنَاهُ إِلَيْنَا قَبْضًا يَسِيرًا ﴿٤٦﴾ وَهُوَ الَّذِي جَعَلَ لَكُمُ اللَّيْلَ لِبَاسًا وَالنَّوْمَ سُبَاتًا وَجَعَلَ النَّهَارَ نُشُورًا ﴿٤٧﴾ وَهُوَ الَّذِي أَرْسَلَ الرِّيَاحَ بُشْرًا بَيْنَ يَدَيْ رَحْمَتِهِ ۚ وَأَنْزَلْنَا مِنَ السَّمَاءِ مَاءً طَهُورًا ﴿٤٨﴾ لِنُحْيِيَ بِهِ بَلْدَةً مَيْتًا وَنُسْقِيَهُ مِمَّا خَلَقْنَا أَنْعَامًا وَأَنَاسِيَّ كَثِيرًا ﴿٤٩﴾ وَلَقَدْ صَرَّفْنَاهُ بَيْنَهُمْ لِيَذَّكَّرُوا فَأَبَىٰ أَكْثَرُ النَّاسِ إِلَّا كُفُورًا ﴿٥٠﴾ وَلَوْ شِئْنَا لَبَعَثْنَا فِي كُلِّ قَرْيَةٍ نَذِيرًا ﴿٥١﴾ فَلَا تُطِعِ الْكَافِرِينَ وَجَاهِدْهُمْ بِهِ جِهَادًا كَبِيرًا ﴿٥٢﴾ ۞ وَهُوَ الَّذِي مَرَجَ الْبَحْرَيْنِ هَٰذَا عَذْبٌ فُرَاتٌ وَهَٰذَا مِلْحٌ أُجَاجٌ وَجَعَلَ بَيْنَهُمَا بَرْزَخًا وَحِجْرًا مَحْجُورًا ﴿٥٣﴾ وَهُوَ الَّذِي خَلَقَ مِنَ الْمَاءِ بَشَرًا فَجَعَلَهُ نَسَبًا وَصِهْرًا ۗ وَكَانَ رَبُّكَ قَدِيرًا ﴿٥٤﴾ وَيَعْبُدُونَ مِنْ دُونِ اللَّهِ مَا لَا يَنْفَعُهُمْ وَلَا يَضُرُّهُمْ ۗ وَكَانَ الْكَافِرُ عَلَىٰ رَبِّهِ ظَهِيرًا ﴿٥٥﴾

وَمَآ أَرْسَلْنَٰكَ إِلَّا مُبَشِّرًا وَنَذِيرًا ۝ قُلْ مَآ أَسْـَٔلُكُمْ عَلَيْهِ

مِنْ أَجْرٍ إِلَّا مَن شَآءَ أَن يَتَّخِذَ إِلَىٰ رَبِّهِۦ سَبِيلًا ۝ وَتَوَكَّلْ

عَلَى ٱلْحَيِّ ٱلَّذِى لَا يَمُوتُ وَسَبِّحْ بِحَمْدِهِۦ ۚ وَكَفَىٰ بِهِۦ

بِذُنُوبِ عِبَادِهِۦ خَبِيرًا ۝ ٱلَّذِى خَلَقَ ٱلسَّمَٰوَٰتِ وَٱلْأَرْضَ

وَمَا بَيْنَهُمَا فِى سِتَّةِ أَيَّامٍ ثُمَّ ٱسْتَوَىٰ عَلَى ٱلْعَرْشِ ۚ ٱلرَّحْمَٰنُ

فَسْـَٔلْ بِهِۦ خَبِيرًا ۝ وَإِذَا قِيلَ لَهُمُ ٱسْجُدُوا۟ لِلرَّحْمَٰنِ قَالُوا۟

وَمَا ٱلرَّحْمَٰنُ أَنَسْجُدُ لِمَا تَأْمُرُنَا وَزَادَهُمْ نُفُورًا ۩ ۝ تَبَارَكَ

ٱلَّذِى جَعَلَ فِى ٱلسَّمَآءِ بُرُوجًا وَجَعَلَ فِيهَا سِرَٰجًا وَقَمَرًا

مُّنِيرًا ۝ وَهُوَ ٱلَّذِى جَعَلَ ٱلَّيْلَ وَٱلنَّهَارَ خِلْفَةً لِّمَنْ أَرَادَ

أَن يَذَّكَّرَ أَوْ أَرَادَ شُكُورًا ۝ وَعِبَادُ ٱلرَّحْمَٰنِ ٱلَّذِينَ يَمْشُونَ

عَلَى ٱلْأَرْضِ هَوْنًا وَإِذَا خَاطَبَهُمُ ٱلْجَٰهِلُونَ قَالُوا۟ سَلَٰمًا

۝ وَٱلَّذِينَ يَبِيتُونَ لِرَبِّهِمْ سُجَّدًا وَقِيَٰمًا ۝ وَٱلَّذِينَ

يَقُولُونَ رَبَّنَا ٱصْرِفْ عَنَّا عَذَابَ جَهَنَّمَ ۖ إِنَّ عَذَابَهَا كَانَ

غَرَامًا ۝ إِنَّهَا سَآءَتْ مُسْتَقَرًّا وَمُقَامًا ۝ وَٱلَّذِينَ إِذَآ

أَنفَقُوا۟ لَمْ يُسْرِفُوا۟ وَلَمْ يَقْتُرُوا۟ وَكَانَ بَيْنَ ذَٰلِكَ قَوَامًا ۝

وَالَّذِينَ لَا يَدْعُونَ مَعَ اللَّهِ إِلَٰهًا ءَاخَرَ وَلَا يَقْتُلُونَ النَّفْسَ الَّتِي حَرَّمَ اللَّهُ إِلَّا بِالْحَقِّ وَلَا يَزْنُونَ ۚ وَمَن يَفْعَلْ ذَٰلِكَ يَلْقَ أَثَامًا ۝

يُضَٰعَفْ لَهُ الْعَذَابُ يَوْمَ الْقِيَٰمَةِ وَيَخْلُدْ فِيهِۦ مُهَانًا ۝

إِلَّا مَن تَابَ وَءَامَنَ وَعَمِلَ عَمَلًا صَٰلِحًا فَأُو۟لَٰٓئِكَ يُبَدِّلُ اللَّهُ سَيِّـَٔاتِهِمْ حَسَنَٰتٍ ۗ وَكَانَ اللَّهُ غَفُورًا رَّحِيمًا ۝

وَمَن تَابَ وَعَمِلَ صَٰلِحًا فَإِنَّهُۥ يَتُوبُ إِلَى اللَّهِ مَتَابًا ۝

وَالَّذِينَ لَا يَشْهَدُونَ الزُّورَ وَإِذَا مَرُّوا۟ بِاللَّغْوِ مَرُّوا۟ كِرَامًا ۝

وَالَّذِينَ إِذَا ذُكِّرُوا۟ بِـَٔايَٰتِ رَبِّهِمْ لَمْ يَخِرُّوا۟ عَلَيْهَا صُمًّا وَعُمْيَانًا ۝

وَالَّذِينَ يَقُولُونَ رَبَّنَا هَبْ لَنَا مِنْ أَزْوَٰجِنَا وَذُرِّيَّٰتِنَا قُرَّةَ أَعْيُنٍ وَاجْعَلْنَا لِلْمُتَّقِينَ إِمَامًا ۝

أُو۟لَٰٓئِكَ يُجْزَوْنَ الْغُرْفَةَ بِمَا صَبَرُوا۟ وَيُلَقَّوْنَ فِيهَا تَحِيَّةً وَسَلَٰمًا ۝

خَٰلِدِينَ فِيهَا ۚ حَسُنَتْ مُسْتَقَرًّا وَمُقَامًا ۝

قُلْ مَا يَعْبَؤُا۟ بِكُمْ رَبِّي لَوْلَا دُعَاؤُكُمْ ۖ فَقَدْ كَذَّبْتُمْ فَسَوْفَ يَكُونُ لِزَامًا ۝

سورة الشعراء